Resources for Teaching

**STUDENT WRITERS AT WORK and in the company of other writers**

**THE BEDFORD PRIZES**
Third Edition

Prepared by

Miriam Baker
Dowling College

Donald McQuade
University of California, Berkeley

Nancy Sommers
Harvard University

Michael Tratner
University of California, Berkeley

A Bedford Book

St. Martin's Press • New York

For information, write St. Martin's Press, Inc.
175 Fifth Avenue, New York, NY 10010

*Editorial Offices:* Bedford Books of St. Martin's Press
29 Winchester Street, Boston, MA 02116

ISBN 0-312-00356-0

Instructors who have adopted *Student Writers at Work and in the company of other writers* as the textbook for a course are authorized to duplicate portions of this manual for their students.

# PREFACE

This new edition of *Student Writers at Work and in the company of other writers* includes prize-winning essays from the most recent two rounds of the Bedford Prize competition as well as reprints of some prize-winning essays from the first two rounds.

Our own classroom experience using the previous editions of *Student Writers at Work and in the company of other writers* has been confirmed by the comments of instructors from across the country; they report that their students have found it both engaging and instructive to read literature written by their peers. The prize-winning essays have provided instructors with more than ample occasions for productive classroom discussions; at the same time students have readily discovered in these essays excellent models for their own compositional efforts. From all accounts, the Bedford Prize–winning student essays have served as the locus for lively conversations and assignments.

Students initially seemed most interested in discussing the content of the essays; they were impressed with what their peers had written about a wide range of often fascinating subjects. Then, as the student users of this book began to develop their own writing and established increasing authority over the distinctive sound of their own voices, they became interested in pinpointing what was particularly effective about each of the prize-winning essays. They not only readily identified the overall rhetorical features of the essays (their distinctive patterns of description, narration, exposition, and argument) but also, and more specifically, came to consider and to understand the compositional and literary elements of the prize-winning essays. In effect, they began gradually to move beyond their work with the structural patterns of the essays and noted such features as the writers' use of generalization, dialogue, tone, figurative language, character, conflict, and the like. The reports of instructors underscored the fact that revision went on continually in their classes as students exercised greater mastery over their own intentions and accomplishments as writers. *Student Writers at Work and in the company of other writers* became a warehouse of writing ideas and class discussions.

The specific classroom-tested process-oriented instructional activities of the first edition were strengthened in the second edition by two major changes. A new chapter, "Moving from Personal Experience to Exposition and Argument," was added to demonstrate the evolution of ideas from expressive writing to the more formal demands of exposition and argument. We also responded in the second edition to the numerous requests of instructors for a companion set of professional essays. The student and professional essays shared thematic interests and often relied on the same compositional strategies to express similar ideas. In this third edition, we have added several new features that extend as well as intensify our attention to the similarities between the approach of student writers and professional writers.

This third edition of *Student Writers at Work* underscores even more emphatically our commitment to making student writing the primary text in composition courses. As in previous editions, we call attention to the most successful features and techniques of each prize-winning student essay, but in this edition we highlight one of these techniques as the basis for an extended instructional unit. Each unit consists of a student essay, an analysis of one effective technique used by the student writer, a professional essay demonstrating the same technique, and suggestions about how students can apply the technique in their own work.

Each student essay is accompanied by a brief but detailed analysis (entitled "An Effective Technique") of what we regard to be *one* of the essayist's most effective techniques. We concentrate on particular techniques from which other student writers can benefit in their own writing. The analysis provided in "An Effective Technique" not only examines the ways in which the compositional technique contributes to the essay's effectiveness but also highlights how other student writers can adapt the technique to their own efforts. The analysis also identifies the specific kinds of writing purposes and topics for which the technique seems most suited. The analysis in "An Effective Technique" thus serves as an instructional bridge to the professional essay or story that follows and prepares students for the specific ways in which the student writer's technique is also used by a professional writer.

Several interrelated pedagogical purposes have guided the development of this new material. We trust that "An Effective Technique" will serve as a model of both effective reading and analytic writing. In addition, we expect that the discussions of specific techniques will increase students' own repertoires of successful reading and writing strategies. It should also convince students that their writing is often distinguished by the same compositional and literary qualities — the same verbal richness and depth — previously attributed only to professional writing. In effect, we hope that the brief analysis following each student essay will encourage other student writers to explore their own special versions of complexity, intensity, and originality.

Each professional essay or story reprinted in *Student Writers at Work* offers a second instructive example of the compositional technique featured in the prize-winning student essay with which it is paired. Focusing on the same technique used by two different writers enables student writers to recognize that they are members of a community of writers and that they share specific techniques with other, professional writers. Each example of professional writing is accompanied by a headnote focusing on the writer's intellectual interests and accomplishments as well as his or her particular approach to composition. Discussion questions follow each professional essay and focus exclusively on the specific compositional technique that links the professional essay to the student essay. Each instructional unit concludes with another new feature, "Working with the Technique in Your Own Writing," designed to encourage students to practice the specific effective technique in their own compositions. We have set out in this new edition to topple the usual barriers that separate relatively inexperienced writers from established writers. Considered together, the student and professional essays demonstrate the seamless web of all writing.

This new edition of the instructor's manual to accompany *Student Writers at Work* continues to offer a detailed analysis of each student essay. In addition, we once again reprint the original assignment that prompted each prize-winning student essay. This offers students an opportunity to see writing as an evolving rather than a formulaic undertaking. As teachers, we continue to be fascinated by the specific ways in which many of the prize-winning authors frequently reinvent topics to serve their own ideas, and while we continue to analyze the rhetorical and literary elements of the student essays, we note thematic as well as compositional connections to other student and professional essays. In addition, we provide suggestions for classroom discussion, in-class writing, and ways to incorporate small group work into composition classes. Following each entry is a précis of the sponsoring instructor's comments about that essay; these reports are rich in pedagogical ideas and practical applications. The comments of the instructors mirror the pleasure many instructors find in working with student writers.

Each of the professional essays and stories that accompany the student essays receives detailed treatment in this instructor's manual. The commentary on each professional essay includes attention to its principal compositional features as well as to the teaching opportunities it presents. We provide additional questions that students might profitably address in class and discuss the interconnections of the professional essay with other selections.

The instructor's manual also discusses the other five chapters of the book — "Student Writers on Writing: An Overview," "Revising Drafts," "Peer Editing," "Moving from Personal Experience to Exposition and Argument," and "Responding to Professional Editing." We explain how we put each chapter together and how to work with each in your classes.

For other teaching ideas, please consult the Suggested Syllabus, the Elements of Composition for the Student Essays, and the Thematic Arrangement for the Student and Professional Essays, which are the final features of this instructional manual.

We hope that this manual will enhance the teaching of *Student Writers at Work and in the company of other writers*. We are confident that students and instructors will benefit from the sense of collaboration and community offered by the range of texts in this new edition.

# CONTENTS

# STUDENT WRITERS ON WRITING: AN OVERVIEW

"Student Writers on Writing: An Overview" highlights the expressive voices of the Bedford Prize winners. The winners describe each phase of their writing and thus offer an inviting and instructive introduction to the composing process. The focus in this and every other section of *Student Writers at Work* is on the process of writing rather than on composition as an abstract subject with fixed limits of information. Certainly the variety of perspectives the Bedford Prize winners offer should help other students realize that there is no single method for writing successful essays. We hope that their comments will also help other students examine their own methods of writing with greater interest and seriousness.

In addition, "Student Writers on Writing" allows students to see themselves as part of a community of writers. These quotations from their peers can reassure students that most writers — no matter how successful they may be — suffer from the same anxieties and fears about writing and share the same satisfactions from writing well. The section makes no claims, however, to be comprehensive and leaves plenty of room for contributions from instructors, students, and even other textbooks.

"Student Writers on Writing" includes a questionnaire on writing printed as an exercise at the end of the chapter, pages 25–26. With the exception of the first question, the section has detailed responses to each question from the Bedford Prize winners. You will find that these students — and your own — have something engaging and teachable to say about every phase of the writing process. The questions can be used, of course, as the basis for either class discussions or writing assignments — the latter in the form of an essay or series of brief essays or perhaps as a series of journal entries. You might want to ask students, for example, to record in writing what they perceive to be their characteristic ways of getting started, writing, and revising. By beginning the course with this inventory of your students' attitudes about and procedures for writing, you will give them a clear reference point from which they can begin to measure their progress. You might ask students to fill out the questionnaire again at the *end* of the semester and have them analyze the differences in their responses. In fact, the students' final essay in the course might well be an analysis of their own work, citing the appropriate evidence from their own essays to document their improvement as well as to remind themselves of aspects of their writing that remain weak and still need attention.

If "Student Writers on Writing" aims to make the act of writing the focus of the class's work, then it is only natural that more time be devoted to listening to how students get started. Our questionnaire sent to the Bedford Prize winners and our survey of the nation's writing program directors emphatically underscore that most student writers have the most trouble getting started. Having your own students describe in writing their special forms of procrastination and their special means for coping with it is a practical way to help them overcome this most obstinate obstacle to writing.

A note on the first question: the exercise on their earliest recollections of writing can serve as the basis for either a productive class discussion or an essay. Asking students to think seriously about their recollections requires them in a certain sense to start from scratch, to examine how their recollections have helped shape their attitudes toward writing over the years. If our experience with this exercise is representative, then most students will recall writing as some form of academic or even parental punishment or pain: for example, having to write "I shall not _____ " 500 times or an essay on _____ for speaking during a school assembly. The variations are seemingly endless — and sadly so.

One useful exercise to help students understand themselves better as writers is to ask them — either in class discussion or in an essay — to create a metaphor for themselves as writers. This metaphor might take the form of an animal (an elephant, a fox, an ostrich), a machine (a bulldozer, a tank, a computer), and so on. It can focus either on the writing process generally or on one of its three phases outlined in the chapter. The exercise can be both instructive and fun, particularly if students read their essays to each other in small groups.

Another fruitful exercise is to ask students to keep a log of their composing process for each of the essays they write. Such an exercise emphasizes that the focus of the course is the writing process — practicing the skills of writing — and not the mastering of an abstract set of rules applicable to every occasion. Keeping track of the different approaches they have used to address different subjects and audiences will no doubt help students appreciate more fully the fact that people think and write at different paces according to their interests and experiences as writers, the requirements of specific assignments, and the expectations of different audiences.

However you present the material in this part, and whatever classroom format you use, inviting your students to talk specifically about their methods of writing will no doubt help them understand more readily — and forcefully — the pedagogical goal of any teacher of writing: to help people exercise the power of meaning and eloquence over the course of their own intellectual lives.

# PART I

# STUDENT WRITERS IN THE COMPANY OF OTHER WRITERS

**HEATHER ASHLEY,** "Leaving Vacita," page 29

**Teaching Strategies**

The assignment that prompted Heather Ashley's essay was an invitation to "expand upon one of the more meaningful things" she had experienced. Ashley's response, like that of Tor Valenza in "At Diane's" (page 549), was to examine a phase in her childhood, a time that had a clear beginning and end where she could mark her growing awareness of "that strange period of the seventies" knowing that "the people who may understand it the best are my peers, because they grew up in the same period."

The opening paragraph begins with a personal definition of a time. To establish the chronology of events, Ashley offers a series of events, both national and personal, that not only allows us to understand the backdrop against which the story of Vacita is to be played but also plunges us directly into her life; we encounter the neighbors, the children, the town, and her best friend along with the author. Students should note the strategy of summarizing the diverse interests of the principal characters. We know them by the books they read, the ice cream they eat, the games they play.

By contrast, the idea of Vacita evolves slowly, marked not by literal time but by metaphor: "Vacita did not emerge over the course of a lazy fall afternoon, nor did it bloom overnight like the apple blossoms. Instead it descended slowly, filling our lives like the red-orange autumn leaves flooded our yards." And just as the idea emerged in leisurely manner, Ashley takes full advantage of a suspended narration. We may be eager to know what Vacita is, but in the tradition of a good storyteller Ashley delays the telling, choosing instead to let us hear the dialogue, see the setting, even enjoy the ice cream — all of which adds to our sense of her childhood. In some ways the friendship between Ashley and her friend is almost more intriguing than the story of Vacita. Her strategy is an interesting one. All too often students start such an essay with a full explanation of some special experience, not sensing the possibilities that narrative offers for building interest and suspense. Not until paragraph 22 does Ashley finally elaborate on Vacita. By then we understand fully the appeal of such an imaginary world because we believe in the reality of the children who have created it.

When students write about friendship, they sometimes have trouble describing the emotional context that gives form to their experience. But in Ashley's essay the characters of the children are fully drawn. We believe as much in their friendship as we do in their world. Watching them stand in the Glen with spears and then suddenly "race home to meat loaf, mashed potatoes, and Sara Lee frozen cheesecake" reminds us continually of the ease with which children move between imagined and real worlds. Readers connect to the world of writers because of such details and just as often fail to connect when such details are absent. But we must be careful to explain to students that it is not the details in and of themselves that matter but the way details are explored that allows us to share fully in their experience.

Another strategy that allows us to construct the experience for ourselves is Ashley's extended use of dialogue in conversation. A second conversation in the essay balances the first. Just as we believed in the evolution of Vacita so we believe in its demise. Ashley lets us hear the hurt and growing boredom that structures her discussion with her friend and, without resorting to generalizations about growing up, she allows us to discover that indeed she and her friend have reached a new maturity. She ends the essay with a repetition of the statement that opens it, changing the verb just slightly: It *had* been the year of Vacita.

## Further Suggestions for Reading, Writing, and Discussion

Tor Valenza's essay offers a natural comparison to "Leaving Vacita." So might Ann Louise Field's "The Sound of Angels" (page 147), which also depicts a time of childhood and the writer's growing awareness of the harsh realities in her life.

As an exercise in limited description, students might be asked to list several episodes or experiences from childhood and then select one from which they draw the characters as fully as possibly, creating conversations they might have had. This can be done in class, using writing groups or full class discussion, to test the emotional reality of the situations they describe. Because this is intended to be a limited exercise, students do not need to offer a full explanation of the situation. For example, a student might wish to describe playing a game with a friend and write about the ritual of the activity, the way they both played, their manner of speaking, where they lived, how many children lived on their block. It is to be a slice of experience mined for the scene itself.

## Instructor's Comments: *JoElaine Retzler Wasson, Cornell University*

The course that produced the prize-winning essay was Writing from Experience, which emphasized not only how to write effectively about one's experience but also how to write for an audience. Each week the students wrote a paper starting at two to three pages in length and moving to five to eight pages shortly thereafter. They chose topics that had to do with important moments in their lives. They were to present to the class not mere journal entries but papers that set scenes through careful description, developed a focus, and ended thoughtfully — not abruptly or too neatly.

At almost every class meeting two students read their papers to the class (often the class had copies of the papers as well). Sometimes after they had finished reading aloud they would notice a number of perplexed faces in the class and say, "Well . . . I guess you had to be there." Right then the authors would know their papers had not worked, for in this class we stressed that through the right amount of detail and inclusion of the author's thoughts and feelings, the audience had to believe, that, if only for a moment, they *had* been there.

The beauty of this class was that the students came to care so much about their papers because they didn't want their lives to come across to others as one big generalization or series of clichés. They learned what a moving paper was and the kind of description, dialogue, and pacing that held a reader's attention.

It is extremely important to declare war on clichés the first day of class and never let up throughout the whole semester. It is too easy to write while on automatic pilot, filling up the page with a lifetime of banalities that are destined to bore the reader into a good snooze.

4

One way to shake a bad case of clichés is to have the students write a paper that uses as many hackneyed phrases, melodramatic moments, and unbearable exaggerations as possible. Have them collect clichés as well (especially from ads and TV programs) and present them in class.

**E. B. WHITE,** "Once More to the Lake," page 39

**Teaching Strategies**

E. B. White's essay is deceptively simple; he orchestrates quite a few disparate elements to create a smooth surface and easy flow. A class might spend a long time discussing all the subtle — and contradictory — impulses that underlie his simple desire to go to the lake. He seems to want to return to his childhood, to nature, to "jollity and peace and goodness," to an "easier time." And he wants to get away from the reality of his restless adult life, perhaps from the big world that is so impersonal and unfriendly. Some students may say he wants to "find himself," since that is often what we think we go on vacation to do.

However, much in this essay contradicts all those simple goals: the last lines of the first few paragraphs suggest that the lake was not merely a comfortable place to him as a child, but rather "remote and primeval" and "like a cathedral." He is partly seeking, in his return, the mystery and wonder that a child felt looking at a place he did *not* know well. Even as a child, White enjoyed the lake because it broke him out of his routines and took him to a magical land. At the end of the essay, he describes the great pleasure a thunderstorm gave him as a child — he liked the scariness of life at the lake as well as its placidity. The lake provided a "safe" scariness. As an adult, he has "become a salt-water man": he turns to the sea to escape. So by going to the lake he is not merely escaping his adult world, but even his adult escape, his adult vacation. As an adult, White needs the sea in all its vastness to give him the same awe of "primeval" mystery that the lake gave him as a child. The adult White clearly has liked the "restlessness" and the "fearful cold" of the sea, but for some reason he no longer does.

To suggest a possible reason why he no longer likes the sea, ask the students what was going on "across the sea" in August 1941 — World War II. The United States entered the war four months after this essay was written. The essay never mentions the war, but one of the differences between the lake and the sea is that the lake is entirely within White's own country: he may wish to withdraw from the contact with Europe that the sea provides. Perhaps he does not mention the war precisely because he does not want to think about it — the war could be the adult horror he wants to avoid. He does mention that what the lake provides is "jollity and peace and goodness," and the opposites of these include war and evil, as epitomized by Adolf Hitler.

White seems to want to escape several other things. Modern technology, represented by an outboard motor's "unfamiliar nervous sound" (paragraph 10), bothers him. His reaction is again complex. He does not want simply to return to nature, without any motors; he wants instead the simpler inboard motors of his childhood. The essay suggests the general point that everyone regards his or her particular childhood world as somehow pure and any changes since childhood as corrupting — so each generation has its own definition of "childhood purity." Note that White's son may very well want to return to the *sea* when he grows up, because the sea will probably represent his childhood vacations. And this son may love the sound of outboards and, perhaps, hate the sound of jetskis.

Moving to a more philosophical level, White indicates several times that he wants to escape time itself. He wants to be the boy he used to be and to be his son. The dizziness in paragraph 5 indicates that he is confused about what he wants.

5

He wants to be the little boy he was once, and he wants his son to be that boy. What is bothering him is that his son is not the same as he, E. B. White, was; the adult White is very aware of the "new generation" that is going to replace him. That awareness explains much of the significance of the last line of the essay. By focusing attention on his son's "vitals" and his own "groin," White makes us think about the physical connections and disconnections between generations. His son is his seed, grown up, although not simply another copy of him. And thinking about generations and procreation leads to thoughts of death. Students might discuss the connections between sex and death: only through sexuality does a race continue beyond the deaths of its individual members; we need sexuality and reproduction because individuals die and decay, and so on. One of the things bothering White may be that his son is about to enter puberty and become sexually mature — a change that always causes parents to feel old because they are being replaced in their most basic function, procreation.

White's desire that nothing change is clearly a desire to avoid facing his own death, because the prime quality of living things is that they change, adapt. The placid lake is an image of death, the ultimate return to beginnings — to the amniotic water of the womb. This essay may be a way for White to begin to make peace with his own aging and death and with the inevitable deaths in the impending war. The twist that a desire for an eternally unchanging world is quite close to a desire for death is a common feature of lyric Romantic poetry (think of John Keats's poetry — "A thing of beauty is a joy forever" in "Endymion" is a sentiment much like E. B. White's and is close to "I have been half in love with easeful Death" in "Ode to a Nightingale"). White occasionally drops into the language of lyric poetry precisely when he wants to create a sense of a frozen moment, a world that appears as still as a painting (as in paragraph 8, "Summertime, oh, summertime, pattern of life indelible, the fade-proof lake, the woods unshatterable").

If students can realize that the strong feeling of this essay is actually formed of contradictory elements, they might understand how the essay can shift tones and yet have one overall feeling. Longing is a complex emotion, full of pain and pleasure: one enjoys imagining something that is not present and dislikes what is present. Students should be able to identify moments in the essay that are painful and others that are very sweet and realize that these opposed moments reinforce one another. The shock of the ending, dipping the reader in the cold water of reality, is important, because the only way to end a reverie is to painfully cut it off. The obscenities in Ashley's essay serve almost the same function as White's mentions of groins and death — they both destroy the illusion of innocence and sweetness and bring the sexuality and death and violence that have been avoided throughout the essay back into the foreground.

## Connections to Other Essays

Several other essays in this collection deal with the clash between reveries and reality, and most of them contain a similar equation of the idealized reverie and childhood that we see in White. The William Hill/Eudora Welty unit on "bittersweet tone" resembles this unit; you could certainly talk about E. B. White's "bittersweet tone." Hill in "Returning Home" (page 233) and Welty in "The Little Store (page 239) use sudden shifts of tone to end their essays, just as White does: all of these writers create the illusion of a sweet world in an effort to forget their current lives, and these illusions simply will not end smoothly. A rather different view of reveries and childhood is provided by James Joyce in "Araby" (page 507). Joyce leaves us uncertain how to react to a boy's idolization of a neighborhood girl. Unlike White's reverie, the boy's reverie in "Araby" may be purely a result of lust and thus not at all a result of childhood innocence. Joyce's narrator does seem to want to escape an unpleasant world — a restricted, inhibited neighborhood — but it is quite possible to see in the ending of Joyce's story that the boy returns to his restricted world harmed by his reverie, forever unwilling to love again. For notes on other essays that focus on childhood, see the instructor's manual entry on Eudora Welty's "The Little Store."

## CELESTE L. BARRUS, "Todd," page 47

Celeste Barrus's essay on the death of her son Todd is in the tradition of John Gunther's *Death Be Not Proud* and William Allen White's "Mary White." Both are elegies to lost children. The Barrus essay may provide difficult moments for discussion because of its highly charged emotional content. It will be necessary to point out that the subject selected itself. When Barrus tried to write a humorous piece, she says, "It just didn't work. I needed to write about Todd." This same point is echoed by Doris Egnor, whose essay "A Life of Quiet Desperation" appears in the first edition of *Student Writers at Work*

Barrus's essay begins with a series of short, flat statements: "Trauma comes to every life. It can leave us helpless." This does not prepare the reader entirely for what is to follow. In fact, it is not the original opening but was added in a later draft. We might wish she had started her essay with the second paragraph ("It began in August"), for this leads us more immediately into the devastating revelation that is to follow. The essay is structured not around a chronology of day-to-day events, but around a careful selection of moments that underscore the reader's growing awareness of Todd's illness. The focus is on a few episodes: the August when the changes are first noted; the evening of the long trip; and, finally, the discovery that began "one muggy morning." Todd's early life and last days are sketched briefly. Barrus's selection of details will demonstrate to students how much an effect can be heightened by winnowing out the less important daily revelations.

The description and dialogue are also excellent examples of the writer's control. With a few carefully selected phrases, Barrus reveals the brutality of the motel owner, "a balding, paunchy man leaning sleepily against the door frame." She also swiftly draws the disparity between the two doctors, pitting unerringly the laconic indifference of Dr. White against the gentle decency of Dr. Haney. Barrus continually uses contrast to her advantage. The reader is struck by Todd's brave decision to walk into the hospital and by his silence as he is strapped to the bed.

In another essay from the first edition of *Student Writers at Work*, Bruce Adams attempts a dual role of participant and witness in his essay "Emergency Room." Yet unlike Adams, Barrus has an emotional stake in the drama. She tells us, "I was acutely aware of things going on around me that day, but as if I were watching from outside my body. I could see myself as I felt — staring vacantly, yet not seeing, knowing what was happening but not participating." Students' attention needs to be drawn to this complex issue. In Adams's piece we do not sense any guilt. In the Barrus essay, the guilt is suppressed by the telling, and we sense that although she needs to tell the story, the narrator has come to terms with her feelings.

### Further Suggestions for Reading, Writing, and Discussion

The dual roles of Adams and Barrus will allow students to examine the differing voices of narrators who write from separate perspectives about somewhat similar topics. Adams is the insider in the hospital; his narrative voice is similar to that of the types he has created. It is the disinterested, objective voice of a spectator. Barrus, in contrast, is deeply involved. She is the outsider who, despite the fact that she manages great restraint in the telling, speaks more directly to the emotions of the reader. You may wish to have students discuss the differences that are uncovered by the respective roles of the narrators. How is the voice in each piece altered by the relationship of the narrator to the event?

A second topic for discussion may be prompted by having students read Theodore Roethke's poem "Elegy for Jane." Ask students to write about or discuss the relationship of his narrator to the event. For example, point them to Roethke's concluding lines, "I, with no rights in this matter, / Neither father nor lover." Contrast that declaration with any one of Barrus's statements about Todd.

Students might also examine the narrative stance in Beverly Dipo's essay "No Rainbows, No Roses" (page 115), with an eye to discovering how the narrator deals with the issue of emotional distance.

## Instructor's Comments: *Karen S. Thomas, Boise State University*

To lead in to this assignment, I read several examples of student narrative essays that I had received in previous semesters. Just randomly, these were all humorous, although I had intended to include some serious examples. Mrs. Barrus tells me she went home and tried at first to write a humorous piece, perhaps about her oldest daughter's dating experiences. She then abandoned this idea because she feels "she's just not a funny person." She knew that she had the Todd story in her, waiting to be told, and that she could remember it and focus clearly on detail, so she began the process of writing that piece.

I was floored by this essay when I first received it — by its control, its detail, its fluidity. I recall reading it for the first time while eating my lunch before Mrs. Barrus's class was to meet. As I read page after page, I was more and more astonished at the quality of the piece. I made *many* positive comments in the margins and returned the piece to Mrs. Barrus with compliments.

The next session I asked her if she would read it to the class. Before class began she agreed. But when it came time to actually read it, she asked me to read it. So I did. Seated before me in class was not only Mrs. Barrus, but also her son Marc, who is mentioned in the essay. I read the essay, feeling increasingly drained, pushing on through one emotionally wracking page after another. By the end of the reading, several students in the room were crying. I stood silently, overcome with emotion, unsure of what to do next.

It seemed we had slipped somehow out of the "frame" of a class and into a different, closer frame — of a family, perhaps? The students congratulated Celeste on the quality of her writing and expressed their sorrow for her. Eventually, I went on with the planned lesson. But it was a day in teaching that I will never forget — a day something happened in the dynamics of the class that has never happened before or since.

Although I cannot prove it, I sense that the reading of Mrs. Barrus's essay had a positive effect on writing subsequently produced by other class members. I feel that some students became more engaged with their own processes of making meaning; they began to write more authentically, finding more "real" things to say. That is, they ceased to view the class as a game for a grade and the writing as strictly for "teacher as examiner," to use Britton's term. In addition, the desire to say something meaningful (intention) promoted the desire to say it well — and their efforts at revision and editing improved.

I believe writing is *meaning,* not correcting, so my advice to students is to focus first and throughout the majority of their writing process on what they have to say. Save editing (correcting) until the final step of writing. I "advise" my students by listening, in a positive way, to their evolving texts and by offering one or two comments about meaning — perhaps a suggestion on organization or a reflection of "Is this what you're trying to say?"

My advice to colleagues for encouraging students to write well is to *be positive*. If all the psychological studies of learning tell us anything, it is that people learn better through positive rather than negative reinforcement. Since writing is at best an anxiety-laden enterprise, instructors have to go out of their way to create a positive environment, an environment in which writing can occur, one that includes trust, security, a willingness to take risks. In conferences with students or in written comments on student papers, always make as many positive comments as negative. I often critique a paper by listing two overall strengths and two overall weaknesses. Then I "correct" maybe half a page as an example of editing. Believe that your students can write. As Frank Smith notes, we expect everyone to learn the far more complex skills of talking and listening; those who don't learn these skills we label autistic. And yet we don't expect everyone to learn to write and read fluently. I try to *believe* my students into existence as writers.

I begin each class session with a quotation about writing, which I have written on the board. I read this aloud and we discuss it briefly. The quotations are by professional writers, rhetoricians, and language philosophers, and they focus on all aspects of writing: that revision for meaning is at the heart of the writing process, taking risks is necessary to produce anything really good, and so forth.

I then give students a topic and have them do ten minutes of freewriting. The topics are taken from ideas for journal entries — anything from a most prized possession to attitudes toward work. I believe these two elements — the quotations and the daily freewriting — are important aspects of my teaching.

## WILLIAM CARLOS WILLIAMS, "The Use of Force," page 57

Williams uses suspense to set up the powerful insights he presents at the end of his story. Discussion of the story can start by exploring the implications of those insights. Williams's narrator is admitting serious flaws in his "good doctor" image. He enjoys attacking the girl and admits that he is acting out of "a blind fury, a feeling of adult shame, bred of a longing for muscular release." One unusual detail is his reference to the importance of "muscular release": we do not often think of doctors as physical laborers. We do sometimes talk about doctors, especially surgeons, as sadists; Williams gives us a clear picture of a doctor enjoying or at least getting a physical release out of dominating and physically hurting his patient.

Williams's story leads to the question of how often people go out of control as a result of pursuing the most moral of goals. People who are trying to do good in the world sometimes become so frustrated that they end up feeling a "blind fury" and "shame" at their inability to make things happen. Williams's "adult shame" may be caused by his inability to win out over a child, but it could be extended to the shame any expert feels when he cannot prove himself superior to those he is trying to help with his expertise. Experts dislike failing and having to try several times: they always want to appear to know just what to do. What happens when experts are frustrated? Can that frustration lead to unreasoning violence?

Once students see the conclusions Williams is leading up to, they can analyze the way he sets us up for them. Williams's doctor explodes into violent action because he is frustrated by his inability to control the situation, and especially because he is uncertain as to what other action he should take. He is in suspense about whether the child is in danger, and this suspense presses on him, forcing him to act. The essay is structured very much like an old western — the hero rides into town to oppose the vicious enemy who has cowed the local authorities. In this case the enemy is a little girl, and the cowardly local authorities who get in the way of the hero are the girl's parents. Williams makes us admire the doctor and the girl for their strength of will.

The essay is set up as a series of battles, building in intensity; we are drawn in by the suspense and the horror, precisely as we would be in an adventure tale. The ending, though, turns on us, criticizing us for enjoying precisely what Williams has set us up to enjoy — violence and suspense. Williams may be criticizing the popularity of tales that give people the vicarious pleasure of being physically violent for a good cause. Westerns and cop shows almost always follow the increasing frustration of the hero until he finally decides that standard, decent methods of fighting evil are too slow and that he is justified in exploding in a fury of righteous action. Williams applies this plot pattern to an unusual topic. Actually, he could be said to be bringing cops and robbers stories closer to home: most of us are not involved in fighting crime, but we all have experience fighting illness and calling in doctor-heroes.

## Connections to Other Essays

You can compare Williams's story to the other essays in this collection written by doctors or psychiatrists about their profession: Richard Selzer's "Letter to a Young Surgeon" (page 300) and Oliver Sacks's "The Lost Mariner" (page 122). Selzer and Sacks, like Williams, write at least in part to criticize doctors. Williams warns doctors of what they are capable of doing as a result of their fury and shame when they do not know what to do. Richard Selzer warns of the dangers of surgeons thinking of themselves as gods. His essay is similar to Williams's in its re-creation of the sheer physicality of surgery and of the horrors that doctors face. Both essays are also about abuses of power. Oliver Sacks portrays a very different kind of horror — insanity — but he too shows the inadequacy and frustration of a doctor. All these essays are, at least in part, arguments that doctors should treat their patients more humanely. Oliver Sacks wants doctors, especially neurosurgeons, to think about their patients' souls. Williams and Selzer show doctors ignoring their patients' feelings in the name of fighting disease. Both writers are trying to make us recognize the role of horrors in our lives and the illusion of control that experts create as a way of trying to deny those horrors.

## JOHNNA LYNN BENSON, "Rotten at the Core, page 62

### Teaching Strategies

Benson's essay was written in response to an assignment that emphasized "learning how to learn." The assignment asked students to "choose something (preferably some idea) from the colloquium that has 'disturbed' you (i.e., somehow moved you, forced you, pulled you, wrenched you, drawn you, excited you, angered you, stimulated you, caused something significantly new to happen to your usual way of thinking)."

With that invitation in mind, Benson seems to have had a wonderful time exploring her own personality in conjunction with a reading in George Kelly's *Theory of Personality*. The essay is structured around a series of questions that Benson addresses both to herself and to an audience she envisions. Preeminently the audience *is* Benson, although she explains how she tested each stage of the process on a classmate:

> I had my victim read for the sense of it, not grammar, though many could not help but comment on grammar. I also asked him to read out loud. That way I could tell if he got the jokes, understood the phrase, etc., without asking him if he noticed it. This technique really helped me in those every

other untyped drafts, because I knew my readers were mainly unwilling and that forced me to rework anything boring, technical, or dead space.

The essay shares some features with Earnestine Johnson's "Thank You Miss Alice Walker: *The Color Purple*" (page 266) and Amber Kennish's "Three Rounds with Dad" (in *Student Writers at Work,* second edition), in which the writers develop arguments from their more informal learning or reading logs. Part of the appeal of Benson's essay is that it allows readers to participate in the discovery of the writer's ideas. Essays of this nature tend to be chatty and discursive; both the reader and writer are encouraged to enjoy themselves.

Benson enjoys playing with platitudes and clichés, which she often turns against herself. The essay begins with an examination of the injunction "know thyself" and sets readers straight immediately. Benson confesses that she has "been beautifully wrong about who I am and who everybody is." Her purpose is twofold: to explain Kelly's theory so that readers will follow her argument and to explain herself in terms of that theory. Paragraph 3 introduces Kelly's central idea, which Benson summarizes and refers to again in paragraph 6. In her description of the essay Benson recognizes the importance of summarizing Kelly's argument: "I spent a lot of time on the third paragraph, trying to explain Kelly without getting overtechnical or breaking the tone. And I spent time on the sixth paragraph trying to find concrete examples to back up the connection between Kelly's theories and my own."

Since it is important for students to learn how to present concisely the thesis of related readings, students might be asked to compare how Benson treats the problem of summarizing a secondary argument with Kennish's redaction of Caroline Bird's essay "College Is a Waste of Time and Money" (in *Student Writers at Work,* second edition). Do the student essays explain enough about the writers so that a reader unfamiliar with the argument can follow the discussion? What kind of information might be added that will facilitate understanding? Students might also examine Margot Harrison's essay (page 201) to see how she helps the reader understand sources behind her argument.

Benson offers numerous examples of the way in which her personality "construct" is at odds with others. She draws on experience, taste, values, and religious beliefs to test her unique spirit. Beginning with paragraph 7 she introduces a dizzying tour of her personality, describing herself as a "chartreuse soap bubble" and then as "an electron carrying practically no weight, fairly indistinguishable from any other electron." The tour proceeds not only as a series of statements but as a series of questions as well. Herein lies a problem. We are not prepared by the breeziness of the opening half of the essay to accept the more serious tone of the second half, in which Benson tests her theological beliefs. Some of the focus for her discussion begins to dissipate, especially in her assumption that all readers will be familiar with Mormon precepts. Students may also need to address the possibility that some of Benson's judgments may offend some readers. How effective are later statements such as "And what about all these other people? I always pictured my intelligence as a chartreuse bubble in contrast with their monochromatic assembly of lemon yellow bubbles. If Kelly gives me the right to be self-made, he also extends that right to all those dumb slobs."

The concluding paragraphs return the essay to one of the reasons for the assignment — to explain how the writer has been changed in some manner by the reading. Benson is more vulnerable in her concluding remarks. A question that students might want to address is how well we are prepared for the conclusion. Might eliminating some of the more gratuitous remarks that appear beginning in paragraph 9 strengthen the complexity of her final point?

Another essay that deals with self-discovery is Patrick Kinder Lewis's "Five Minutes North of Redding" (page 320). Although what the reader learns about

Lewis is inferred rather than stated, comparing the essays will give students an opportunity to consider what the writers discover about themselves.

### Further Suggestions for Reading, Writing, and Discussion

A simple but necessary task for revision deals with opening and concluding paragraphs. Students should take one essay that they have written and excerpt these two paragraphs, placing them side by side, and ask if the paragraphs might be interchanged. In other words, might the conclusion as easily serve as an introduction? If the paragraphs were to be reversed, what changes would occur to the essay? On the other hand, if the conclusion has taken the writer quite a distance from the beginning, how well does the middle of the essay support that journey? What steps does the writer need to take in the body of the essay to prepare for the changes at the end? A student essay that might be useful for this exercise is Terry Burns's "The Blanket Party" (page 76).

### Instructor's Comments: *Brian S. Best, Brigham Young University*

I suppose the most important single bit of advice I give to students is to be sure that what they write matters to them. I often tell the anecdote of Robert Frost's meeting a freshman class, collecting their papers, asking by a show of hands who in the class really cared about what they had written, and then, when no hand went up, dropping the whole batch in the wastebasket with the remark "When you care about what you've written, I'll care enough to read it."

I think the varied and interesting subject matter of the course matters a great deal in the writing part of the course. Too many writing courses try to get interesting writing from students without supplying them with enough interesting reading and discussion.

### LEWIS THOMAS, "The World's Biggest Membrane," page 71

### Teaching Strategies

Students often think of metaphors as decorative devices to make writing "literary." An exercise might help students see that a metaphor can structure an essay. Select a simple metaphor, such as "The football player rose to the occasion, becoming a lion on the field." Then have the students list as many qualities of lions as they can — fierce, animal, large, hairy, big feet, tends to eat the weakest prey, and so on. Add any words or ideas that are associated with lions — tiger, circus, symbol of Dreyfus Company, Exxon tiger, cats, purring, wet noses. Now ask the students to try using these related terms to describe the football player. They could write an essay about a football player, repeatedly using metaphors related to lions to describe different aspects of the player: he roars and is fierce on the field; he is rather a gross fellow with big, hairy feet and an ugly mane of hair; he turns the game into a circus, without discipline; he stuffs himself silly at each meal, then practically falls asleep, purring like a fat pussycat. Exploring a metaphor can help students discover new ideas and can unify an essay containing disparate ideas.

Thomas uses "membrane" and "breathing" as metaphors throughout his essay, bringing in many related terms. Consider the different kinds of "membranes" he speaks about: "covering" and "uncovering" (paragraph 1); "screened out" (paragraph 3); "filters" and "penetration" (paragraph 7); "greenhouse" (paragraph 8); "roof" (paragraph 12). Similarly, "breathing" turns into "respiratory mechanism" in paragraph 5; "cycles" in paragraph 8; "strangling" in paragraph 9 — and even "transact this business" in paragraph 2 (exchanging money is like exchanging oxygen).

Thomas's metaphors allow him to write lively, amusing prose while presenting a large amount of information in a short space. Students might list all the information and all the different theories that Thomas includes and consider how memorable the essay would have been if he had merely described "objectively" the scientific theory of the development of oxygen and the atmosphere. Thomas sets the tone of his piece in his first paragraph by describing the earth, viewed from space, as "astonishing." He constantly changes perspective, from the moon to a long-distance view of the earth to the inside of a cell to life forms millions of years ago — along the way stopping off to bring in images of banks, pools, ponds, greenhouses, and secure roofs. The complexity of Lewis's metaphors is probably most apparent in the second paragraph, where he seems to be discussing a "cell" in scientific, objective language. Yet he speaks of cells "poised," as if they had good posture and then uses "you" to personify cells. What "you" have to do if you are a cell is "hold out against equilibrium, . . . bank against entropy, and . . . transact . . . business with membranes in our kind of world." He sounds like a financial planner talking about how to survive a depression. Similarly, in the discussion of Berkner's theory in paragraph 6, Thomas talks about an "explosion" of life and "biological inventiveness"; war and brilliant munitions designers enter the essay. Since Lewis has to rely on metaphors to explain scientific theories which themselves are metaphors, he ends up using metaphors to explain metaphors.

## Connections to Other Essays

Thomas works to make us have feelings about the atmosphere. His goal of personalizing and humanizing something we usually think of in nonhuman terms bears many similarities to arguments for a more human view of human beings themselves in "The Lost Mariner" by Oliver Sacks (page 122) and "Letter to a Young Surgeon" by Richard Selzer (page 300). Sacks and Selzer believe that doctors too often regard human beings the way most of us think of rocks and air. These writers are trying to encourage doctors to treat human beings humanely, an attempt that might seem to have more merit than trying to make us have humane feelings about the atmosphere. However, Thomas is also a doctor, and students might consider his view of the atmosphere as an extension of a doctor's view of human beings. Furthermore, in recent years the environmental and ecology movements have begun recognizing the earth as a single living organism (a concept called Gaia). Ecologists think that seeing everything on earth (including all people as well as rocks and air) as part of one living creature can have extensive political and social consequences. (For further reading on this idea, suggest the book *Gaia*, by ex–NASA scientist James Lovelock, which has sparked controversy in recent years.)

Aldous Huxley's essay "Words and Behavior" (page 103) argues that people should never personify abstractions and should refer to "real" things in precise, concrete terms. Huxley's argument sounds as if he is against metaphors, but his essay is full of them. Students might have a good discussion about whether Huxley would criticize Thomas's essay. The answer is far from clear. Huxley and Thomas do seem to disagree about what kind of language is most "scientific," and this disagreement may reflect recent developments in science. In Huxley's day, there was still a hope that science would achieve the rigor and precision of mathematics and logic, based on solidly established facts; recently that view has been largely abandoned. Thomas thinks, as the headnote indicates, that science should no longer be taught as a field that piles up established "facts."

**TERRY L. BURNS**, "The Blanket Party," page 76

## Teaching Strategies

Terry Burns's essay was written in response to assignment 21, "Eye-witness Account, Human Subject," from James Moffett's text *Active Voice.* The assignment reads: "Tell some incident that you witnessed that involved other people; you were observer not participator. Recreate it as you saw it and include the reactions you had at the time."

What is especially interesting about Burns's essay is the opportunity it offers for a discussion of narrative stance. Although the assignment calls for the dual role of observer and witness, Burns assumes the more difficult task of being a witness in the biblical sense. The essay is laced with his judgments and interpretations of what others might be thinking. For example, Burns points to the hypocrisy of the men — "everyone pretended to be asleep" — and to Sgt. Slat's cold-blooded inspection — "If any concern showed on his face it was certainly not for Goodrich." Encourage students to discuss the issues raised by these comments.

The writer attempts a difficult point of view, a shifting perspective between subjectivity and objectivity. He has tried to establish a third-person narrator. At no point does the word "I" appear, yet we are aware that the narrator has been involved in some manner in the event. Class discussion might center on the choices Burns made to achieve this unflinchingly moral focus. Instructors might ask how the story would be changed if the narrator were to speak in the first person. The original assignment does not necessarily ask the writer to assume a third-person narrator, yet Burns does. What is lost or gained by the use of the third person?

Some good opportunities for questions arise. What was the narrator's role during the event? Does the distance achieved by the third person mask some of the narrator's own guilt at being a passive witness? What are the realities of intervening in such a situation? It might also be interesting to compare the narrative role used by Thu Hong Nguyen in "A Good Woman" (*Student Writers at Work,* second edition). Nguyen also writes in a seemingly dispassionate way about the role of women in Vietnam. Like Burns, she uses a personal experience — in this instance her outrage at the treatment of her mother — to get at the larger issue of cultural approbation for acts of cruelty against the individual.

The essays by Burns and Nguyen point to a central issue for the composition class. While many of the essays in the text deal with autobiographical matters, the opportunities are numerous for exploring these papers for the more traditional expository writing assignments. For example, "The Blanket Party" begins as a personal narrative and leads to a generalization about the misleading nature of the goals of military life. The initial essay might easily be incorporated into a research paper that illustrates or classifies abuses of military life. The incident might be the focus in a paper on examples or a comparison and contrast essay — what one is promised by joining the military and what one finds. It is important to point out to students that all good writing must begin with a compelling purpose.

Burns's concluding generalization is the overriding reason for his telling of the story. In his student questionnaire Burns comments that he began by "trying to show how easily young men can be manipulated into a criminal act just to make things easier for themselves. I don't think that was what the military was supposed to teach." Furthermore, he uses the Goodrich story "to stay away from military jargon and dwell on the petty problems of basic training." Thus the narrative itself helps to focus the issue and lends support to his generalization. As instructors we add strength to the purpose of exposition if we allow time for a natural evolution of subject matter from its personal or subjective beginnings into the more difficult demands of formal discourse.

14

Part II, Chapter 3, "Moving from Personal Experience to Exposition and Argument," offers several examples of how students can mine a personal-experience essay for an assignment on argument.

## Further Suggestions for Reading, Writing, and Discussion

Two short fiction pieces that might provide an interesting comparison with Burns's essay are James Moffett's "The Suicides of Private Greaves" (in his *Points of View: An Anthology of Short Stories* [New York: New American Library, 1966]) and Ralph Ellison's "Battle Royal." Moffett's story deals with the indifference of army officers to the obvious emotional breakdown of a young soldier that ultimately results in his suicide. Ellison's story, which later became the first chapter of his novel *Invisible Man,* addresses the violence and hypocrisy to which the narrator is treated prior to delivering his high school graduation address.

A third possibility of comparison is "A Frozen Night" by John Ross Thompson (*Student Writers at Work,* first edition). Thompson's essay addresses an instance of a solitary soldier's cruelty toward a fellow soldier in Korea.

Several essays in the text deal with aspects of rituals. Students might write about some incident that they either took part in or witnessed and that raised questions about their own behavior or indecision at intervening.

## Instructor's Comments: *Robert Durante, Canisius College*

After teaching composition for eight years, I find myself spending more time on freewriting and peer group work. If instructors emphasize the process of writing as much as their course time permits, students will have the maximum opportunity to improve their writing skills. I try to emphasize this process in two ways. First, I sequence my writing assignments so that each essay prepares students for subsequent papers. Second, I emphasize process within each writing task by employing peer conferencing groups. Normally, I will give my students seven to ten days to produce a finished paper. After we discuss the requirements of an assignment, students will have four to five days to write a rough draft. They bring the draft (along with two copies) to their peer group session and work in groups of three — so each student will have two responses to his or her essay. (My students and I find the checklist in *Student Writers At Work* [first edition, pp. 242–243] a valuable means by which to evaluate any type of writing.) After the peer group work, students have another three to four days to revise the essay and hand it in. I always make clear that students may meet with me individually during this period to discuss their essays. In addition, they have the opportunity to revise their essays again after they are graded and returned. I think Terry benefited from this process because he produced three separate drafts.

## GEORGE ORWELL, "Shooting an Elephant," page 82

## Teaching Strategies

Orwell's essay is a fine example of the interplay between story and theme (or thesis). The essay is actually structured much like the standard essay students often write: introduction, thesis, body full of specific details, conclusion. Students should be able to analyze how all the parts of this essay function by applying what they already know about essays. The opening two paragraphs use two standard strategies for introducing a topic. The first paragraph presents a little anecdote that leads into the topic of the essay — imperialism — and hints at the views

Orwell will ultimately present. The second paragraph presents a series of common generalizations about imperialism, simplistic views that the rest of the essay will modify and qualify. Orwell thinks that imperialism is bad, but that is too simple a point for an essay — everyone knows that. The second paragraph is a variant of the standard opening for an essay in which the writer says what "most people think" and then moves to complicate or counter those conventional views.

Orwell's thesis appears in the second sentence of paragraph 3, in the form of a very general description of the point he wants to make in the rest of the essay: he will tell an incident that will show "the real nature of imperialism — the real motives for which despotic governments act." Some instructors might not want to call this a "thesis" since it does not state Orwell's main point directly — it does not tell what the nature of imperialism is. Some instructors use the word "contract" for this kind of statement of theme — Orwell is contracting with his readers, promising to deliver something in the rest of his essay. More important than what we call this statement is considering how it functions. It gives us a framework to interpret everything that follows. Orwell is telling us how to read his story; we are to search through it for the "real nature of imperialism." The body of Orwell's essay is one long story, but that does not mean that there is only one large point in the whole essay. Students usually think of the body of an essay as consisting of several main points, each supported with its own evidence, examples, and stories. But a writer can use one long story to make several main points, as Orwell does. The various points about imperialism do not come sequentially, as points in a standard essay do. Rather, readers can interpret various elements in the story as revealing various aspects of imperialism. The three basic players in the drama — Orwell himself, the crowd, and the elephant — can be interpreted in several different ways. Orwell seems a representative of imperialism, but we have two choices for what or who represents the colonial nations. If we consider the crowd as the colony, then Orwell seems to be saying that imperialism becomes despotic because one nation pretends to be superior to another and must act violently to stop the inferior nation from laughing at this silly pretense. Imperialism is then like bullying, an act performed by someone who wants to appear strong but doubts his own strength and so picks on weak opponents.

If we interpret the elephant as a symbol of the colonial nations, we get a slightly different conclusion: imperialism is frightened of the power of the colonies, which could squash the empire like a "toad under a steamroller." The essay could express the sense that the colonies are starting to "go mad," to rise against the British powers. Orwell may even be hinting at the thought that ran through many British minds as colonies revolted, that perhaps the only solution would be genocide — kill all the colonists or, symbolically, kill the whole elephant. The colonies are also in this interpretation "natural" powers, while the British rulers are weak men supported by technology (rifles) but with little natural dignity.

Each of these interpretations can be developed much further in class discussion by considering details in the story. A third possibility that may not have been intended by Orwell might be interesting to discuss: the elephant could represent the empire and Orwell could be shooting at the empire by writing his essay. In paragraph 2, Orwell says he did not know that "the British Empire is dying," and in the story the main image of something dying slowly is that of the elephant. If the elephant represents the empire, it is something that is extremely powerful but that has gone insane. Instead of turning its power to serve the colonists (as imperialism first dreamed of, bringing the benefits of technology and modern government to "backward" lands), it is killing them. Orwell shoots the elephant to try to halt the horrors of imperialism.

Orwell's conclusion focuses strongly on the first interpretation — the crowd as the colony and Orwell as the imperialist. His main conclusion seems to be that imperialism becomes despotic to avoid revealing its foolishness. But Orwell still

16

relies on his readers to expand that conclusion into some larger idea about why imperialism inevitably makes its rulers afraid of appearing foolish. Students can discuss the advantages and disadvantages of leaving the thesis implied in an essay.

Students might comment that even though Orwell is against imperialism, he still portrays the Burmese stereotypically. His next to last line — "I was very glad that the coolie had been killed; it put me legally in the right" — seems quite close to a defense of imperialism. His conception of legality is entirely a British imposition on the Burmese culture; he seems to have less concern about loss of Burmese life than about maintaining his own position, even though he admits he acted immorally. Isn't this close to saying, "The system is terrible, but I am glad that it gives me a good job, even if others had to die"? Another ambiguous line is in paragraph 2: "the British Empire is . . . a great deal better than the younger empires that are going to supplant it." It may be speaking of communism, nazism, or the colonies that achieve independence. In any case, he seems to be saying that the British tyranny is better than Russian, German, or Burmese tyranny, and so he seems to be at the least ethnocentric.

## Connections to Other Essays

"The Use of Force" by William Carlos Williams (page 57) also presents a small anecdote about a man in a position of authority being driven by his own shame and anger to violent action. Williams does not promise a general insight into a whole social system, but his essay certainly makes us think about power (of doctors, of adults).

"Words and Behavior" by Aldous Huxley (page 103) criticizes Britain and its symbols of power and glory much as Orwell's essay does. Huxley's analysis of how people fool themselves into believing that their criminal desires are moral acts in defense of their nation could easily be applied to Orwell's story. Students might consider these questions: "How does imperialism drive Orwell in his job as government authority to personify abstractions and depersonify human beings?" and "How does Orwell present the 'reality' behind the false abstractions and depersonifications that support imperialism?" Orwell has himself written an essay very much like Huxley's — "Politics and the English Language" — which also could be used to analyze Orwell's own writing.

"I Forgot the Words to the National Anthem" by James Seilsopour (page 472) shows the experience of a person living in a country where he and his family are treated as less than human; he in a sense presents the Burmese side of Orwell's essay. Students could discuss how much this point of view is present or absent in Orwell's essay. Seilsopour's title suggests that he is presenting a critique of nationalism that is similar to Orwell's critique of imperialism.

**CURTIS CHANG,** "Streets of Gold: The Myth of the Model Minority," page 90

## Teaching Strategies

Curtis Chang wrote his essay in response to a series of carefully defined instructions. The essay, the final assignment for his composition course, was to be "a convincing, well-documented, engaging essay in support of a clearly defined proposition or claim." Chang was instructed to use at least six documented sources for the paper, including "human sources" such as interviews. The paper might begin with an illustration or anecdote, but the proposition itself was to appear by the first or second paragraph.

It is clear that one of the strengths of the essay derives from the clarity of the purpose. Chang has a firm idea of what is expected from the paper. But perhaps even more important, Chang is exploring a subject in which he has a personal interest. Generally, when students are asked to argue a point of view, the hardest aspect of the writing is the difficulty of formulating their convictions. Classroom assignments often ask students to take a position that does not necessarily interest them. Thus the argument seems artificial and the discussion sometimes suffers from a formulaic treatment. *Student Writers at Work,* however, contains examples of fine papers that should be of interest to students precisely because the writers explore subjects that have personal value. As instructors, not only is it important that we give clear and incisive instructions for the writing of an essay, but it is also crucial that we help students uncover a way into the essay, either by encouraging them to select a topic that is compelling to them or, in the case of a given topic, to find a unique means to engage them in the discussion. Time spent in the class discussing this issue is time well spent for both the student and the instructor.

Chang's connection to the argument is evident in the opening sentence of the essay: "Over 100 years ago, an American myth misled many of my ancestors." The first paragraph offers a quick explanation of the myth. Readers do not have to wade through a detailed account of the background. This is important to note for students. Chang trusts that his readers will be sufficiently familiar with the role of Chinese laborers and the myths of getting rich quick in America in the nineteenth century so that he can move swiftly to a discussion of the way the myth seems to be reasserting itself as a contemporary minority success story. The device of listing key publications and headlines is also an economical means of pointing out the pervasive nature of the misconception.

By the second paragraph, we are quite clear about the proposition. Students should note that getting firm control of an argument early in its development increases reader confidence. To help readers follow his argument, Chang narrows the discussion to what it means to "make it" in America and then points to the statistic of median family income, which appears to be the basis for the assumption. Again, Chang exerts considerable control. This might be a good point at which to discuss how to limit an argument in an essay. Having swiftly established the broader background — the myth, then and now; the pervasiveness of the myth in the media; the definition of the myth — he will now concentrate on the erroneous nature of the statistical basis for the assumption.

Chang then examines a second fallacy, "Asian Americans' educational status at 'the top of the class,' " thus bringing further support to his central thesis that it is dangerous to make assumptions about people as a group. He gives equal weight to the second part of the argument, finally arriving at a redefinition of the model minority as "a perfect model of racial discrimination in America." Here again is an opportunity to ask students what effect that assertion might have had on them had it appeared at the beginning of the argument. It is important for students to become aware of the strategies for creating consensus in a persuasive essay.

Given the impressive array of documentation that Chang selects, we should stress that he keeps the focus primarily on evidence drawn from well-respected newspapers and magazines, which in itself lends authority to his viewpoint. He does not scatter the discussion by examining myths from other areas of the media. What he introduces in the first two paragraphs he delivers consistently throughout the paper. One quibble we might have is that he touches only briefly (paragraph 24) on the contribution by Asian Americans to the mythology. Students very often worry about admitting a point that might seem to weaken their argument. One purpose for presenting information that seems to undercut the central point is to allow the reader a role in the reasoning process.

**Further Suggestions for Reading, Writing, and Discussion**

Ha Song Hi's "From Xraxis to Dzreebo" (page 216) contains references to " 'anti-alienism, re-emergence of white supremacist groups, scapegoating of Asians for failures of the domestic economy, and heightened tensions between minorities over competition for jobs.' " The essay also directs considerable energy at United States policy toward Mexicans. Although the purpose of the essay is different, the point about bias is the same.

James Seilsopour's "I Forgot the Words to the National Anthem" (page 507) also addresses the effects of prejudice on its author's life. While racial or ethnic bigotry seems fairly apparent, students often suffer from other forms of bias. Students might consider how labeling — learning disabled, handicapped, words pertaining to weight — affects their self-image. Ask students to write about times in their life when the use of a name or an epithet made them feel uncomfortable or ostracized. The assignment might begin by compiling the various ways we attach labels to people and by reminding students that they frequently refer to classmates as "jocks," "wimps," "princesses," and so on, in casual conversation.

**Instructor's Comments: *Judith Beth Cohen, Harvard University***

The most helpful advice faculty can offer: help students find topics that excite them, that are sufficiently limited and accessible that they can do some original work. If it is a subject close to their own lives, they can find people to interview and will be energized to work harder on research. Having something important to communicate to peers or to the community at large can provide a good incentive for revising an essay. Using actual documents and talking to real people help make assignments live.

Focus on their writing process. Something as seemingly trivial as changing where they sit when they write or the fact that they can discuss ideas with a roommate can come as a startling insight to students. Think of ways they can draw on the topics they are studying in other courses for your assignments so their studies can be more integrated.

Bring writers and journalists to class to talk about how they get ideas, how they find sources for a controversial story. Demonstrate that writing is a real-life activity and not something confined to the classroom.

Share your own writing struggles with the students. Bring in a project you are working on.

**ALDOUS HUXLEY,** "Words and Behavior," page 103

**Teaching Strategies**

Huxley identifies two basic ways people use language incorrectly: "personifying abstractions" and "depersonifying human beings." Students might confuse these two "errors" and might think they cancel each other out. If politicians want to forget that individual people are involved in wars, and so "depersonify" people by speaking of abstractions such as "force," why do the same politicians strive to make us think of individuals by personifying countries? The trick is to see that by making these two errors, people may choose when they want to think of individuals and when they want to think of abstractions. Huxley is showing us that talk of abstractions and talk of individuals can be substituted for each other when it is convenient. The "individuals" that we like to think about when we go to war are not really human beings, but rather gods and demons who cannot actually be killed because they transcend the particular human bodies that we kill in wars. The "individuals" that we do not like to think about are the ordinary folks who are blown up by bombs. The two linguistic errors allow us to turn warfare between masses of ordinary individuals into fights between a few giant superindividuals.

Huxley recognizes that he is discussing a rather abstract subject and is in danger of falling into the same linguistic errors he criticizes. In his last paragraph, he says that the only way to speak morally is to talk and think about problems "exclusively in terms of concrete reality: that is to say, of persons." Every abstraction and every imaginary superindividual must be translated into terms describing physical, concrete reality. Huxley does this throughout his essay, creating vivid pictures of masses of persons being blown up and making us think of nations as millions of individuals, not as single entities.

To keep us grounded in concrete reality, Huxley also uses specific, familiar images to explain his complex analyses. For example, in the first paragraph, in trying to analyze how language alters behavior, he says that language brings continuity to life and reduces animals' tendency to simply follow every random emotion. Then he brings in, rather unexpectedly, a little scene of a cat interrupting a fight to "hoist a hind leg." Besides being amusing, this familiar image makes his point clear — animals cannot concentrate continuously on one task for very long. Language, he claims, allows us to continue fighting even when we want to go to the bathroom. Huxley intends to be somewhat ironic in this image — he would be delighted if humans did get distracted from their wars. Language makes humans different from animals; it can make them better or worse depending on how it is used. Huxley adds into his image of a cat fight a small hint of the way humans become worse than animals: he describes the cat's lifted leg as "a more than fascist salute." Huxley elaborates on this hint in the rest of the essay, where he analyzes how humans misuse words to serve their worst animal instincts, to become fascists who seek to slaughter entire ethnic groups.

Throughout his essay, Huxley repeatedly drops in familiar images to ground his abstractions. After reading this essay, we carry these images with us as much as we carry Huxley's complex argument. We remember the lady with the dueling cats, the lady with the toasting fork, the muskets and sabres fighting without any people involved, and the fool who tries to put out a fire with a "colorless liquid that happens to be, not water, but petrol." Huxley's images carry the emotional weight of his argument; they are sometimes horrifying, sometimes amusing. Without these images, the essay would be dry and hard to understand. Some readers may feel that he has not used enough images, that this essay is still rather stuffy and abstract. That reaction may be a result of a change in readers — Huxley wrote before TV provided a way for images to constantly accompany words. We may rely on images in our thinking now much more than anyone did in Huxley's day.

## Connections to Other Essays

Huxley's analysis of the ways people use words to falsify reality could be applied to several other essays in which we see persons using official or traditional language to justify immoral acts. Students could examine the way "personified abstractions" and "depersonified human beings" lead to cruelty in "On Killing the Man" by John Clyde Thatcher (page 515), "The Old Chief Mshlanga" by Doris Lessing (page 522), and "Shooting an Elephant" by George Orwell (page 82). Orwell has also written an essay — "Politics and the English Language" — like Huxley's "Words and Behavior," about the moral consequences of the misuse of language.

The Declaration of Independence by Thomas Jefferson (page 286) is a political document full of the "linguistic errors" that Huxley criticizes. Students might consider, after examining the Declaration, whether it is possible to inspire people to join any political cause without using Huxley's "linguistic errors."

**BEVERLY DIPO,** "No Rainbows, No Roses," page 115

Dipo's assignment was to write a detailed description of an emotional experience. She says that her description of the death of Mrs. Trane "almost wrote itself."

In her notes, Dipo explains her decision to sidestep any melodramatic opening — "I am a nurse and I work the night shift" — yet she also wanted to establish credibility for the impersonal viewpoint she adopts. When we examine the opening paragraphs we discover the remarkably neutral tone of a trained professional who accepts the probability that her patient will die that night, who can watch with "detached, medical routineness" the "skeleton frame," the arm "taped cruelly to a board," "the uneven . . . Cheyne-Stokes respirations." We suspect that these observations are not rendered without compassion, but there is distance between the nurse and the patient sustained until the moment the narrator stops looking at the patient and begins to touch her.

In the fourth paragraph, the tone softens. The act of touching itself shifts the focus for the detail: it is less clinical, more tender. For the few moments that remain, the narrator enters the seeming emptiness of the woman's life, speculating on her graceful hands and the life they might have held. What seems paradoxical at first is that the narrator who attends the last moments of Mrs. Trane has never seen her prior to that evening. Yet in the brief time that she spends with her patient the essay becomes a portrait of the narrator as well. As readers, we learn more about the nature of death because of the extraordinary ability of the narrator to extract meaning for us.

Question 7 in the section "Focusing on Beverly Dipo's Techniques and Revisions" helps with the conflict the narrator experiences about what constitutes growth. Is it sustaining the "detached, medical routineness" that is at the heart of her training, or is it the humanity of holding a dying patient's hand, witnessing and accepting "the life force which continues despite such a state of decomposition"? Paragraph 6 does seem to veer, if briefly, from this fine balance that the narrator has achieved, particularly at the moment when a single tear slides down Mrs. Trane's cheek and the narrator cries in response. Yet who can deny the truth of such a moment, no matter how close it moves to the melodrama that the writer wants to avoid? It is at this point in the essay that the narrator explains more fully what the experience means to her emotionally. It is also here that the underlying purpose for the writing is stated. In some ways we do not need the concluding paragraph (paragraph 7), although it does place Mrs. Trane in the larger context of her long and useful life. Students might want to consider how the essay would affect them if that paragraph were omitted. Also the title may not seem appropriate in light of that paragraph. Students might consider what other possibilities exist for a title. So often titles, final paragraphs, or final lines undercut the purpose for the writing. These are good places for students to edit carefully in their own writing.

For a discussion of how Beverly Dipo explored "No Rainbows, No Roses" to develop a second essay, "A Time to Die," see Part II, Chapter 3, "Moving from Personal Experience to Exposition and Argument."

**Further Suggestions for Reading, Writing, and Discussion**

In the first edition of *Student Writers at Work,* Joanne Mente in "Home Is Where the Heart Is" describes how her father's disease affects her family. This also skirts sentimentality and yet offers insight into the realities of the dying. It would be a particularly useful essay to discuss with Dipo's composition.

The subject of death is usually difficult for students who have had their share of suffering but would prefer not to encounter it in the classroom. One story that deals with the issue of suffering in a way that seems to offer some resolution is James Baldwin's "Sonny's Blues." It is a long story and a difficult one, but finally it is almost cathartic from a student's point of view. While it does not entirely address the issue raised in Dipo's essay, it may allow students to look at the ways we try to avoid suffering. As Baldwin says, "No, there's no way not to suffer. But you try all kinds of ways to keep from drowning in it, to keep on top of it, and to make it seem — well, like *you*."

### Instructor's Comments: *Joyce Kinkead, Utah State University*

My students work in conferencing groups. When they are reading drafts of essays, I encourage them to comment on where the writing works especially well. They are to note specific instances in the essay that are especially good and also to let the writer know what parts don't work as well and why. After that, they pass the papers around to check for errors.

I use the small groups in many of the warm-ups also, having the students write group anecdotes or share mini-assignments for use of voice. I also bring in examples of my own writing for their critiquing, plus let them know how much I rely on peer critiquing.

Many instructors see small group work as chaos. The key is structure. Although the room may seem noisy, students actually work on the task, provided they are given structure. One of the best ways I've found to have successful peer editing is to do a model critique with the entire class, using a sample essay and asking them for response. Students are rather afraid of the group responses until we've done this. If the students are simply told to get in critique groups and edit each other's papers, it will be a failure.

I think the only way to teach writing is to have writing as the text of the course. We analyze a lot of student writing, and I lecture very little. I didn't learn to ski by reading a book about skiing; I learned to ski by getting out on the side of a mountain. I want my students to do the same thing. Yes, they are going to fall down sometimes, but my job is to be there to pick them up and encourage them to take more risks with their writing.

One of the best ways we've found to stimulate interest in writing is to publish our own student anthology. Students really like reading other students' writing, and they see their own work published — a real surprise for them.

### OLIVER SACKS, "The Lost Mariner," page 122

### Teaching Strategies

Students will probably find Jimmie's case history fascinating and horrifying, and they may be put off at times by Sacks's references to intellectual theories. Sacks refers to quite a few writers by their last names, as if his readers were already familiar with them. The significance of most is made clear in context, and we have footnoted explanations of the four names that might mystify students — Buñuel, Hume, Bergson, and Kierkegaard. It might be useful to tell students that they do not need to know anything about the philosophers, about Buñuel's movies, or about brain surgery to understand the essay.

It would be a shame to give students the impression that this essay is difficult to read, because Sacks's philosophical musings can be discussed in down-to-earth terms. Students need only consider these questions: "Why does Jimmie's case challenge our notion of what it means to be a human being?" and "Why does Sacks doubt whether Jimmie has a soul?" Then class discussion can move to the question of whether scientists, especially neurosurgeons who analyze the brain, should or should not think about human souls. Someone might bring up artificial intelligence and computers — do computers have souls? If *Star Trek: The Next Generation* is still popular, the character Data bears comparison to Jimmie; in some ways Data is the exact opposite of Jimmie — a machine with too good a memory — but the question of whether Data has a soul is equally difficult to answer.

David Hume's concepts might arise in discussion of these issues; the quote from Hume in paragraph 63 is quite understandable. To help students imagine "Humean being," ask them to focus on the flow of words and images in their brains to see if they can regard it as a random flow, with no unity at all. Is the image each of us has of being a unified person merely an illusion?

To turn the discussion to writing strategies, ask students how Sacks would have presented this material if he had been writing for a scientific journal. He would have excised the scenes, the dialogue, and the portrayal of his own emotional reactions. Yet these elements are essential to Sacks's argument: he wants to show that "empirical science," which deals only in hard facts, not in emotional reactions or human interactions, cannot adequately deal with Jimmie. If scientists do not see Jimmie in a setting such as a church service, they will fail to see what is most essential — his soul. Scientists who restrict themselves to empirical phenomena, to the physical properties of Jimmie that can be measured and catalogued, will never see that Jimmie still has a life that is worth living.

Sacks argues in his last paragraph that the "aesthetic, the moral, the religious, the dramatic" have a place in science. He therefore must make his writing at least partly aesthetic, moral, religious, and dramatic. He wants to prove that scientists cannot avoid dealing with all the vagaries of beauty, morality, and the soul. In fact, when scientists treat persons as collections of measurable phenomena, they essentially reduce people to "Humean beings," to a bubbling froth of unrelated elements, failing to see the "soul" that ties the elements together. Sacks has to write scenes and dialogue to show the "I–thou" relationship he had with Jimmie and to avoid the "I–it" relationship that most scientists establish with the people they study.

## Connections to Other Essays

For some thoughts about the similarities among all the essays in this collection written by doctors, see the notes on William Carlos Williams's "The Use of Force."

Sacks's essay provides a somewhat philosophical view of the importance of using scenes and characters in essays. Students can also look at his scenes and characters as strategies for winning a debate about the nature of human beings. In that light, Sacks's essay could be placed in the units on scene and character in this collection, those centered on David Landmann's essay "The House" (page 309) and Dianne Emminger's essay "The Exhibition" (page 138). Students could compare Sacks's presentation of Jimmie and Landmann's presentation of Isiah Lewis as arguments for the full humanity of persons who do not speak or think in the "proper" way.

## DIANNE EMMINGER, "The Exhibition," page 138

An important subject in the composition class is the study of definition. Students often struggle with these assignments, resorting to dictionaries or thesauruses for answers that are generally unsatisfactory to everyone. A more interesting and less constricting means of introducing definition is to allow the class to explore terms from their own perspective using personal experience to rediscover the meaning of ordinary words. In effect, finding their own distinctions allows students to uncover naturally the many shades of meaning, the denotative and connotative aspects of language that often baffle inexperienced writers. Emminger's essay addresses the definitions of art and appreciation.

Emminger is at her best when she describes the crowds that walk about an art gallery, developing through her portraits of "pearl-draped elderly women" and "unkempt, long-haired men and sandal-footed women" a sense of the pretentiousness of art appreciation. Against the artificial setting of the gallery, she presents the innocence of a small child delighted by a rainbow. While the idea is hardly new, Emminger manages her definition ably by working through a series of contrasts, playing the patrons of art against the paintings, the child against the spectators, and finally nature against art.

Emminger is less successful in her almost heavy-handed description of the natural form of raindrops in paragraph 4. Here she falls prey to her own indictment of studied comment. Also, at times she overstates an idea, especially when trying to convey the naiveté of the child: "Her eyes gleamed like the lights. Such innocence was in this child." Students might want to consider, as part of this reading, how to give fresh meaning to clichés. A good writing exercise would be to describe such words as "innocence" or "pleasure" without stating the obvious. For other interesting treatments of descriptive detail, see the essays by Heather Ashley (page 29), Ann Louise Field (page 147), William G. Hill (page 233), and Paula Sisler (page 496).

## Further Suggestions for Reading, Writing, and Discussion

Class time may be used to have students quickly draft their definition of an abstract term. Limit the list to two or three words such as "beauty," "loyalty," "friendship." After five or ten minutes of writing, ask students to discuss their definitions, encouraging them to debate the merits of their versions. As an extended assignment students could take the initial draft and develop it into a full-blown argument, based on personal experience, much in the manner of the student writers in the book.

A good reading to accompany "The Exhibition" is Richard Wilbur's poem "Museum Piece." Ask students to compare Wilbur's point with that of Emminger, either in a class discussion or a paper. Another comparison can be made with W. H. Auden's poem "Musée des Beaux Arts."

## Instructor's Comments: *James Rosenberg, Point Park College*

First of all, Dianne Emminger earns her conclusion. The central perception of the essay is common enough, and it would have been easy for the writer to state the terms of her contrast (organic child versus static art) and let it go at that. But the writer is tenacious in detailing what she saw (the motion in the raindrops, the child's head, the child's fingers) and thus the "unsophisticated beauty" is shown rather than asserted. The essay explores, rather than summarizes, the experience.

The essay is also written in more than one voice, which makes it unusual among student writings. Its tone is at times prosaic, it is playful in the second paragraph and conversational in the third. In the final paragraph the writing becomes formal and argumentative. The writer's versatility shows her controlling the material rather than filtering impressions. And Emminger is able to control tempo by means of placement of clauses, so that the essay becomes energetic as it moves from bewilderment to resolution.

24

One further strength of this piece is the way the comparison of gallery patron with artistic subject is established in paragraph 2. Emminger consciously tries to blur the distinction between the watcher and the watched. It is central to the author's intent that the child and the art be seen as competing possibilities, and Emminger introduces that twinning in the second paragraph with the gallery of portraits. It is noteworthy in student essays, or in any essay, really, to find a writer introducing a perception by showing the actual perception rather than stating it as a truism.

I used the essay in class. I began by asking what a "gentle thing" was in the essay. I took this word from the first sentence because I wanted to show how the essay was not about any child but about a particular one: a child who was tactile, not self-conscious, and not judgmental. After we talked about how the essay defined "gentle" and "simple" through the child, I asked what in the essay was not gentle. After receiving the standard replies ("connoisseurs") and the imaginative ones ("the unkempt," "the dejected") I asked if the narrator in paragraph 3 could be described as gentle or not gentle, according to the comparison in the essay. I wanted to show, first of all, how the experience written about was not just something "out there" but rather something that was happening to the narrator. Once we talked about how the narrator herself was unsatisfied and distracted, I tried to show, by discussing what the child meant to the narrator, that the conclusion was something learned rather than something already known.

I chose this particular way of proceeding because I thought it important to present the essay not as a virtuoso performance but as a useful piece of work. The class was able, through talking about the conclusion as something learned, to state that their admiration for this essay came not only from how "right" it seemed but also from how the writer worked to make the experience hers.

## ANDREW WARD, "Yumbo," page 143

### Teaching Strategies

This essay divides neatly into three sections, two small scenes framing a section of general argument. The two scenes are amusing, if not downright silly, but they seem appropriate for Ward's serious point, because he is criticizing the silliness of fast food product names. He wants us to feel not only that these names are silly but that they serve an insidious purpose — "to convert an essentially bleak industry, mass-marketed fast foods, into something festive."

Ward does not show us the wicked "management" of these fast food restaurants, the people who are using silly names in such an underhanded way. Instead he portrays the people who work in such restaurants and who appear in their ads as idiots — uneducated, slow-witted, "bug-eyed and goofy." He creates characters who are the "fronts" for the management, and these characters are essentially silly names personified — silly persons.

Against these persons Ward pits Kelly Susan and a "tidy little man" — thoroughly serious, sane, sober persons. However, Ward does not present these persons as perfect; he mocks them as he mocks the restaurant personnel, though not as viciously. By mocking everyone in his scenes, Ward can make his case without appearing to be a nitpicking humbug himself. Ward seems aware that to protest vehemently against fast food names is itself rather a silly thing to do, and probably only stuffy people would do so. Kelly Susan and the "tidy little man" are not completely appealing characters. We imagine the nightly battles at Kelly Susan's house when she tries to convert the rest of her family to her vegetarianism. And the man seems to protest too much and to achieve at most a Pyrrhic victory, since he ends up going hungry for refusing to say a word.

25

(text pages 147–157)

Students might discuss whether Ward is actually a bit out of control when he mocks the characters who represent his point of view. Is he perhaps aware that he is making a big deal over nothing? Is he actually a stuffy fellow like his two protagonists? Why does Ward even go into these restaurants if he dislikes their language and their food?

## Connections to Other Essays

Ward's use of rather silly persons to represent both the people he dislikes and the people he agrees with is a fairly standard tactic of satire and often leads readers to wonder whether the author has any opinion at all or merely wants to mock everything. Allison Rolls in "Lady Diana: He Married the Wrong Woman" (page 426) and Alice Kahn in "Pianotherapy: Primal Pop" (page 433) also write satire in which it is difficult to tell how serious the writers are. Ward's position is clearer than theirs because Ward's own voice stays fairly reliable and free of self-mockery, especially in the discursive paragraphs in the middle of his essay. Rolls and Kahn present themselves as unreliable narrators.

Diane Kocour in "The Diet Industry Knows Best — Or Does It?" (page 272) writes about a topic fairly close to Ward's; both authors focus on deceit in the food industry. Students might try to imagine these two authors switching styles: Ward writing an impassioned attack against McDonald's, Kocour using a series of satiric scenes to expose the manipulation of the diet industry.

## ANN LOUISE FIELD, "The Sound of Angels," page 147

## Teaching Strategies

The assignment for Field's essay grew out of a piece by Susan Allen Toth, "Nothing Happened." The assignment asked students to write about some aspect of life in the town where they grew up: "You may decide to tell a number of stories as Toth has done, or you may decide to write at length about a single memory. Of course you won't be able to capture all aspects of your youth, nor of your home-town, but you can, as Toth, catch edges of it in prose. Whatever strategy you choose, be sure that your piece gives us some sense of your younger self and of the particular town or city or rural area that you called home."

Field responded to the essay by choosing to recall a series of activities that she shared with her older brother, Brett. This is an admirable and tautly chilling piece of writing that never sentimentalizes or indulges in self-pity. The first half of the essay re-creates the hero worship many of us have known, the eminently satisfying relationships that children establish to protect themselves from the realities of their lives. Despite the almost lyric descriptions of devouring doughnuts and steal-ing oranges, readers sense quite early that the writer will reveal some central tragedy in the abandonment of childhood play. It is not unlike the feeling we have in Barbara Carter's essay "Momma's Cupboard" (*Student Writers at Work*, second edition), which depicts the children lined up like "paper stacking dolls" at the pantry door. We sense there is a darker side to the narrative.

The oranges become the central symbol. Whereas in the first half of the essay the forays into the orange grove represent the freedom and power of the two small children released from the constraints of obligation, by the time the narrator has discovered the real reasons behind the "camping trips" the oranges assume a more sinister reality. This is, however, not just a reflection for its own sake. Underlying the narrative is a discussion of poverty and its debilitating effects on the entire family. Field does nothing to save the reader from her pain: "As our house came into view on the walk home I saw it as if for the first time. The paint was peeling and the yard was overgrown with bushes and ivy. From inside the house I could hear two people yelling at each other. I saw my whole life in that frame; my hand-me-down clothes that had been Brett's before mine and somebody else's before his, and my used and shabby bike with rust and dents under the cheap blue paint."

The essay is beautifully balanced between its two halves — the description of the first part and the explanation of the second. Paragraph 6 summarizes what has come before: the orange groves, the sankies, the lyric appreciation of an outdoor world where no adult concerns intrude. But in the ensuing paragraphs and the dialogue Field introduces the larger issues of the essay appear. This is an essay about growing up, about the exigencies of adolescence that force two children apart, about the anger and despair that no amount of playing can disguise. At no point in the essay do we discover that Brett is now dead, but we can well imagine that the fact of his death must have prompted the depth of Field's memories and have caused her to reflect that "revising this paper was like cutting off bits of my arms and legs."

The essay is also rich in well-chosen, telling details that Field combines with the natural ease we see in Carter's essay. Students should notice how descriptions differ when the point of view shifts. For example, in the Curry essay the narrator stands outside the experience whereas Field and Carter view their experience as participants. A class discussion might center on the degree of intimacy or distance that is created by the various narrative stances.

### Further Suggestions for Reading, Writing, and Discussion

David Landmann's essay "The House" (page 309) describes a family living in a cardboard shack in the middle of an affluent urban society. Julie Reardon in "The Unmarked Road" (Student Writers at Work, second edition) narrates her experience with poverty as a young adult. These essays provide numerous opportunities for examining how different writers, given a similar assignment, treat narrative stance, details, description, and underlying generalizations.

Paula Sisler's essay "The Water Lily" (page 496) also deals with the dissolution of a family. Unlike Field, Sisler does not entirely prepare us for the ending. Students might discuss the differing strategies the writers use to bring about their final generalizations about family life.

We have all admired someone immeasurably when we were children. You might ask students to describe their particular "hero" and pick one or two instances that symbolize the meaning of the relationship for them. Another approach to this assignment is to have students write about the subject from a dual point of view — that of a child and that of themselves as adults.

### Instructor's Comments: *Nancy Jones, University of Iowa*

What I hope for all my students is that they will find their own reasons for writing, so that once the course is over (and before it is over) they won't need me or any other teacher to prompt them to write. The only way to "improve" one's writing, I believe, is to write and write and write. And, of course, to think and live fully — though such general advice is not usually what students want to hear if they frame a general question of "What can I do to improve my writing?"

To my colleagues I would say, "Let the students write, and let them see that you also write and that you value it highly." I share my writing with students a couple of times during every course, so they can see my own struggles with words, my own deliberations about revising. As to the matter of "letting students write" I provided the context for Ann to write the essay which we then submitted to the

Bedford contest. I asked the kind of question which would allow her to tell a story she had been wanting to tell for a long time. The art of asking good questions is a central concern of any writing teacher, I would hope, as well as the correlative art of learning to hear what the student-writers are saying (so you will know what to ask them next to help them develop their thinking, clarify their feelings, explore that inkling of an idea that is just emerging).

I occasionally use journals in my writing classes as places for students to jot down ideas or to write brief (sometimes directed) comments on readings we've had for the day. Sometimes I ask them to think about a particular issue we'll be discussing (in a classmate's paper or in a published essay) and write about it before the discussion. At other times I ask them to bring together what to them were the most important points of a discussion after it was over. I consider the journals the students' property and never ask to see what they have written there (though I offer to respond to any entries they'd like me to see and respond to). Likewise, I never ask that they share their entries with one another. If they choose to do that on their own, that's fine. But I feel that they should make that decision themselves — so they come to see that in certain contexts they can write whatever they choose and can remain in complete control of what happens to that writing.

My students often work in small groups, but only after I have taken the class through several large group workshops of student pieces. I try to show them the kinds of questions which are most fruitful in *describing* (rather than evaluating) a piece of writing. So we work at talking about what is happening in a piece and what strategies the writer has used to accomplish what he or she has accomplished. I suggest that the students also comment on what they perceive as the strengths of the piece, followed by any questions they might have. Only toward the end of the semester do workshop discussions turn to issues of editing or of suggestions for revision. (I feel that it is most important for students to know how their writing is perceived/described by other readers and that they come to think of ways to make their writing more effective, closer to fulfilling the purposes they had in mind. We don't talk, then, about *better* writing, but rather *more effective* writing when we come to talk about revisions.)

## JAMES BALDWIN, "Notes of a Native Son," page 156

### Teaching Strategies

James Baldwin's essay is full of "revisions" in his views — of his father, of whites, of himself. To help students see all the different revisions, you might ask them to see how many different ways they can fill in the blanks in this sentence: "Baldwin had thought _____, but then he realized _____." Sometimes Baldwin can quickly state a change in his thinking: in the second paragraph he tells how he stopped thinking of the "apocalypse" as a mystical event and came to see it as the quite real horrors of a race riot. And sometimes he needs pages to describe how his attitude changed: in the first section of the essay, he describes the year he spent away from home, where "I had had time to become aware of the meaning of all my father's bitter warnings. . . . I had discovered the weight of white people in the world" (paragraph 6). To take us through this complex revelation, he first loops back in time to show us his early views of his father and of whites and then tells the story of the incidents in New Jersey that revised those views.

The entire essay encompasses several changes in the way that Baldwin viewed his father. The first third of the essay sets us up to believe that Baldwin's father was a cold, paranoid man, perhaps justly so because the world was cruel to him and to all blacks. The ending revises that image, revealing that the father had a kind, decent side to him. The final revelations are somewhat surprising; however, if we look back at the beginning, we find plenty of evidence of Baldwin's admiration for his father. Baldwin is ambivalent about his father from beginning to end, but he moves from trying to deny all the good in his father, trying to maintain a great distance between them, to feeling very close to his father and discovering in his father's words "a meaning which had never been there for me before" (paragraph 45).

Baldwin's revision of his image of his childhood and his parents takes him in a direction opposite to Ann Louise Field's. Field at first sees her parents as wonderful and then discovers their flaws; Baldwin starts off seeing his parents as awful and discovers their goodness and intelligence. Field loses her innocence and bemoans its loss; Baldwin in a sense rediscovers his innocence and finds a way to maintain it as an adult. Field seems to end up in a world without benevolent deities or authorities; Baldwin returns to religion, to a trust in the Lord and in his father. Students might discuss whether their own experiences growing up are closer to Field's or to Baldwin's. Some students might comment that they have undergone both kinds of change at different ages: first they believed in their parents as gods, then, perhaps around puberty, they saw them as flawed persons who had little to offer, and finally in college (or even later) they regained some sense of their parents' wisdom and goodness.

Part of what causes both Field and Baldwin to revise their family views is their growing awareness of social issues and of how those issues intersect with their families' lives. Students might try to analyze in writing how their own families have been affected by social phenomena and social issues. Some students may feel they cannot write an essay about such a topic because their families have not been involved in social problems such as poverty and racism. But such students can write about the influence on their families of middle-class status (or real wealth). They could also write about how having few contacts with other races affected their families. Stories by F. Scott Fitzgerald and Sinclair Lewis might help students see how to present rich or middle-class people as products of their social background.

## Connections to Other Essays

John Mason, Jr.'s "Shared Birthdays" (page 388) traces, as Baldwin's essay does, a man's reactions as he goes to a funeral. It is written in a similar structure, starting just before the funeral and using flashbacks to fill in the past up to that moment. Mason is also writing about a rediscovery of a good part of childhood.

For notes about other essays that focus on childhood and growing up, see the instructor's manual entry on Eudora Welty's "The Little Store." For notes about other essays that focus on minority and immigrant experiences, see the instructor's manual entry on Maxine Hong Kingston's "The Woman Warrior."

## BONNIE HARRIS, "The Healing Power of Music," page 176

### Teaching Strategies

Bonnie Harris notes several stages in the drafting of her essay that will be of interest to students. First it is clear that she has "discovered" a subject she wants to explain to her fellow students as well as to herself. And, like other writers who have found a fascinating topic, she had problems not only with the scope of the information she uncovered but with creating an order that would at once persuade and inform an audience that "would probably not be as interested as I was in the technical aspects of music healing, and in fact might need some convincing that there really was such a thing."

She describes the second stage of the composition in this manner:

I wrote an outline from my notes on dozens of books and articles I'd read, from conversations I'd had, and from the workshop that originally inspired me. The outline and the first draft went through a peer critiquing process in my composition class that encouraged me to focus more on specific examples of how music is used for healing and its contrast with traditional medical practices. My original ideas needed to relate more to how my audience could possibly benefit from the information I had to offer. My second draft changed focus accordingly and then required a lot of judicious editing to condense the original ideas down to a manageable size to go with the material. I had to cut out a lot of what I considered to be interesting but extraneous stuff.

Harris is faced with a problem quite similar to that of Thomas Leyba (page 335). Both essays seem to overwhelm the writers with information that begs to be included in the discussion. A comparison of how each writer addresses the problem might provide a good lesson on organization. Despite the fact that Harris did not have time to write a third revision, she seems to achieve her ideal of an essay that is at once informative and persuasive.

The theme of the essay is established economically in the opening quotation. Each subsequent paragraph offers further qualification, illustration, and synthesis of the argument. Harris moves easily back and forth between examples of ancient forms of healing and modern scientific applications, providing excellent "road signs" for the direction of the discussion. By the time we read paragraph 6 we are ready for the more technical discussion that follows. Terms such as "resonance," "entrainment," and "oscillation" have been defined carefully. Clear examples of the terms have been provided — both technical and ordinary; the reader feels at ease with the terminology. Harris returns frequently to earlier assertions before introducing new ideas, thus making the reader a full partner to the discussion. She is also at ease with citations, which she generally simply asserts and notes in the body of the essay. Where the information is a bit more complex, she explains the source of the information, such as the reference to Peter Hamel in paragraph 11. We are always able to follow the origin of the idea to its application. This is a point that might be made as part of the class discussion of the essay.

The essay offers a wide range of connections that seem easily accomplished, thus emphasizing the success of the organization of ideas. Students would do well to examine this essay for examples of control and coherence.

## Further Suggestions for Reading, Writing, and Discussion

Diane Kocour's essay "The Diet Industry Knows Best — Or Does It?" (page 272) is another example of an argument that is clearly ordered and persuasive. It would be interesting to have students outline both Kocour's and Harris's essays describing what each paragraph does rather than what it says. Kenneth Bruffee explains the concept in *A Short Course in Writing* (Boston: Little, Brown, 1980, p. 36): "The purpose of a descriptive outline is to help inexperienced writers become more critically aware of what they are doing when they write. It is a device which can help writers become more conscious of the complex mental operations they perform in writing, and especially more conscious of the relationships among the several parts of an essay."

To create a descriptive outline, students write one sentence explaining what the paragraph "does," that is, what function it serves in the essay: describe, narrate, list, explain, trace, compare, analyze, synthesize, hypothesize, give background, project, reason, etc. To explain what a paragraph "says," students summarize or paraphrase in one sentence what the paragraph contains.

As a class exercise, let students describe what each paragraph attempts to do and what each paragraph "says." Then ask them if they see other means of ordering or developing ideas. There is real benefit to allowing them to look at other students' writing with an eye to uncovering structure. It is an exercise in distance that writers do not always follow in revising. As Bruffee suggests, "The descriptive outline is not an aid to writing. It is *an aid to rewriting*. It is the closest thing in writing to what in mathematics is called a 'proof.' It is a way writers can check to see if they have written what they think they have written."

As a further exercise, students might like to apply a descriptive outline to one of their own mid-process drafts. Encourage them to see where they are skipping from function to function, where they might combine paragraphs, where they need to add information. If, for example, students offer a complex proposition and give only one example, you can prompt them in a neutral manner to see the gap in their argument. The value of the descriptive outline resides in its "neutral" stance because it does not judge the content; rather it allows students to label what is present and what is missing, much in the way an architect must look at a structure to see that it achieves its purpose.

## Instructor's Comments: *Joan Waters, University of Alaska*

Students need to learn that revision is the norm, not the exception, for all writers. For this reason, I require at least one revision of all major assignments in composition. I emphasize that even strong essays can be improved and encourage them to produce their very best writing, no matter what their initial skill level. Less advanced writers often have major content or structural changes to make on revisions, while more skillful writers focus on polishing their style.

I use a peer response system which I call "nonconfrontational" editing. I have peer critiquing pairs respond to typed drafts of each major assignment, but they use peer critiquing forms instead of conversing directly with the student author. Each pair of students responds in writing to the essays of any two *other* students during the class session in which the paper is due. Meanwhile, their papers are being critiqued by other pairs across the room.

I never have students directly exchange papers, for I have found that they tend to be more open and honest in their comments if they are not confronted by the defensive author during the process. However, authors may talk with their respondents after the process is completed to clarify comments or ask for further suggestions. We practice constructive criticism on anonymous papers before they start responding to each other's papers, so they learn that the purpose of the response process is not to grade their peers but to give other student authors helpful ideas about how to revise drafts.

## JOYCE CAROL OATES, "On Boxing," page 187

### Teaching Strategies

Joyce Carol Oates knows that many people who read her essay will be against boxing. You might begin discussion of this essay by considering her criticisms of those who hate boxing: she calls such people "liberals" and implies that they are racists. She also suggests that these people hate boxing because it reveals what they do not want to believe — that all civilization is based on and depends on violence.

To counter the standard arguments against boxing, Oates shifts the grounds of her discussion in a surprising way: she does not consider boxing as a sport, and

31

she does not view it as having entertainment value (she says she does not "enjoy" boxing at all). She defends boxing as much more important than sport or entertainment, as a literary work that expresses something we must pay attention to. By "reading" the actions in a boxing ring the way we might read a story, she shows us how boxing can reveal truths that we need to see. Students might try to state the various truths that Oates says boxing reveals. A partial list: the greatest persons will inevitably decline from greatness (paragraph 9); strength underlies civilization (paragraph 13); the disenfranchised in society are angry (paragraph 14); nature is outside of language (paragraph 15); fathers can save battling sons (paragraph 18); man's greatest passion is for war (paragraph 29); men can love only after fighting (paragraph 28); we need savage rites but cannot believe in them anymore (paragraph 33); the individual is supreme over technology (paragraph 39).

If students can see how Oates generates these varied insights, they can adapt her methods to their own topics. Partly she looks at boxing from many different perspectives: she considers boxers (1) as two universal individuals confronting each other; (2) as part of a family scene; (3) as representatives of social classes; (4) as Americans; (5) as "writers" creating stories; and (6) as priests enacting a religious ritual. Students could look at any sport in these different ways. Consider baseball: (1) The pitcher-batter duel is usually described as two individuals confronting each other. (2) Many terms describing baseball suggest a family drama — "visitors" coming to your "home"; the "infield" is like the yard surrounding "home," while the "outfield" is like the undeveloped land nobody can live on. (3) Baseball has been racked by concern about racism throughout its history. (4) Baseball is certainly an "American" sport — perhaps because it conjures images of little towns on the edge of the wilderness full of boys throwing balls to each other. (5) Baseball might be best compared to a novel rather than a drama, since it is divided into innings, like chapters, each of which can contain its own crises and climaxes. And baseball allows for quirky characters and individual idiosyncrasies, as a Dickens novel does. The "story" a baseball game tells is different from the "story" a boxing match tells. Baseball perhaps tells of heroic individuals working for a greater glory, building civilization in the wilderness (finding a way to "go home," to get out of the fields). (6) We worship certain baseball heroes as gods (Babe Ruth, Joe DiMaggio).

## Connections to Other Essays

Several essays in this collection center on masculine competition as Oates's essay does: "The Right Stuff" by Tom Wolfe (page 353), "On Killing the Man" by John Clyde Thatcher (page 515), and "Arm-Wrestling with My Father" by Brad Manning (page 369). Wolfe's and Thatcher's essays focus, as Oates's does, on the connection between death and masculinity. Oates defends the masculine involvement with death and violence. Thatcher is opposed to the myth that physical violence is an essential part of becoming a man. Wolfe is ambivalent, relying on ironic distance to allow himself to admire and mock violent, competitive men. Wolfe and Manning provide interesting variations on Oates's point that masculine confrontations are a way of communicating without words. Oates seems to regard boxing as predating language, as touching on some primitive, natural way that humans could interact. Manning seems to regard his father's need of "physical language" as at least in part a defect, a lack of ability to speak directly. Wolfe makes much of the astronauts' never discussing directly what the "right stuff" is, but it is difficult to tell whether he admires it or not.

**MARGOT HARRISON,** "Creative Transfiguration from the Death of a Moth," page 201

## Teaching Strategies

Assignments that ask students to compare essays often produce rote or formulaic analysis, partly because we tend to teach comparison and contrast as an isolated rhetorical strategy rather than one of many that a writer may employ in any given piece. Thus when Margot Harrison was asked to compare any two essays that had a common theme (in this case the essays deal with insects), her instructor added a bit of useful advice: "Remember that your paper should use the texts to say something — it shouldn't be a simple catalogue of similarities and differences."

Harrison approached the assignment with an interesting question in mind: "The goal of my essay was to carry out an effective comparison, specifically to prove that the two essays, written in different time periods by very different authors, deserved to be compared at all." This is an important point. Often students approach such an assignment by assuming that the essays must be comparable — after all the instructor asked them to compare them — which in turn encourages them to act as recorders whose sole function is to pigeonhole or tally up various items. Instead Harrison asks the essays, Virginia Woolf's "The Death of the Moth" and Annie Dillard's "Death of a Moth," to prove to her that a comparison is in order.

She begins by looking at the titles, trying to infer an initial similarity, and then introduces a definition, Wordsworth's "spot of time," to focus her discussion. What is so beguiling about the essay is the care and leisure with which Harrison examines discrete issues. Too often in such essays, students begin by listing and then compound the problem by describing rather than interpreting what they have listed. Harrison asks what is the difference between the use of *the* and *a* in the titles, drawing distinctions about the way in which the "spot of time" is "framed and depicted."

Harrison's examination leads her to discover differences in the writers' narrative stances. This is a rather crucial issue for teaching such essays. Students generally have a difficult time with viewpoint, particularly when both essays seem to be written in the first person and when both narrators seem to be speaking about personal experience. By examining each writer's treatment of first-person narrator, Harrison infers two distinct purposes, which she illustrates with well-chosen quotations from the texts.

Particularly impressive in her strategy is the solid manner by which she arrives at her final point. She moves carefully from an initial examination of the difference between the titles to a contemplation of narration to a discussion of tone and imagery, concluding that both essays are statements about art and transfiguration. Even the title of her essay implies that a "text has been created from another text," something that so rarely happens when we make these assignments. Too often the analysis seems to be imposed on text rather than creating a new text that stands on its own.

## Further Suggestions for Reading, Writing, and Discussion

Ask students to read Harrison's analysis without reading the related essays by Woolf and Dillard, which are located elsewhere in the text (pages 397 and 330, respectively). Class discussion might center on how much students are able to infer about the essays without direct knowledge of them. Are they able to follow Harrison's argument? What strategies does Harrison use to help her readers? Then you might ask students to read both essays and discuss how Harrison's essay affected their reading.

Since comparison essays are a staple of the composition course, an in-class writing might center on taking very brief passages, perhaps only a sentence or two, from any essays that are assigned and asking students to look at discrete elements as Harrison does, noticing pronouns, kinds of verbs, tone, imagery. The exercise is aimed at making students more at ease with textual analysis and less concerned with global issues.

## Instructor's Comments: *Leonard Cassuto, Harvard University*

I allow my students to revise as often as they like — within reason. I figure that if they're willing to write it, I ought to be willing to read it.

I try to teach my students that essays, like all good writing, are creative.

I favor extremely flexible assignments that guide without directing. The longer the assignment, I find, the more exact the result the teacher has in mind. Such expectations can be constricting, making the work into an exercise rather than an essay.

## PATRICIA HAMPL, "Defying the Yapping Establishment: *Under the Eye of the Clock*," page 212

### Teaching Strategies

Hampl's essay is an example of a writer establishing her own voice while respectfully telling us about another writer. The review is full of quotations, but we do not ever lose our sense that Hampl is leading us through those quotations. The essay begins with a quote from Nolan's book, but the quote is not Nolan's first line. Hampl is not merely telling us what Nolan thinks is important in his book; she is showing us what she thinks is important. Her opening paragraph shows that she is more interested in this autobiography as an act of writing than as a tale of a person's life. She even ends her first paragraph with her own aphoristic generalization: "Frustration is implicit in any attempt to express the deepest self." Note that she ends her entire essay with another such line of her own about the act of writing: "His voice speaks, as a writer must, from the margin, the solitude where detachment encounters all the jangled emotions it must serve." Hampl frames her review with these sentences, which seem to express her own experience as a writer. We see Nolan's book as an example of Hampl's ideas about what it means to be a writer.

Hampl's focus on this autobiography as a piece of writing determines the organization of her review. The first feature of the book that Hampl considers in detail is its style. When she moves beyond style, in paragraph 8, she turns to a physical description of "the act of writing" and then to Nolan's sense of the task he faces as a writer. Even when Hampl turns to telling us about Nolan's family (paragraph 10), she says she is discussing them only to further prove that Nolan is "a true writer." She ends her brief comments on Nolan's family with a quote about how his father gave Christopher a "merry love of writing." Hampl has read this book as a fellow writer and a fellow autobiographer. Students might imagine a very different review written, perhaps, by someone who simply enjoyed the events Nolan narrates and did not focus on the book as an example of writing.

In the last section of this review, Hampl does focus on the story Nolan tells. Hampl aims at the end to create an emotional reaction in her readers by re-creating the sad yet triumphant conclusion of Nolan's book. Students might discuss whether she is giving too much away. Nolan set up his book to create suspense, to make readers wonder whether he will succeed in school. Hampl destroys this suspense, telling us that Nolan eventually quits school. Is she treating the book with great respect, as a work worthy of reading over and over again, even after one knows what is going to happen? Or is she reducing our pleasure in reading Nolan's autobiography, and not respecting what the author is trying to do?

Hampl compares Nolan's book to many different kinds of literature. Students may not be familiar with such things as "picaresque novels" or the "Joycean" manner of writing, but they should still be able to see what Hampl is trying to do in these comparisons. She writes for an audience that values great literature. Students might consider what comparisons they would use in writing reviews for a college, or even a high school newspaper.

## Connections to Other Essays

"Knife Used" by Christopher Nolan (page 461) is a chapter from his autobiography. By reading that chapter, students might be able to evaluate how well Hampl has introduced Nolan's book to them.

## HA SONG HI, "From Xraxis to Dzreebo," page 216

## Teaching Strategies

Ha Song Hi's assignment invited an unusual response to writing from a source. She was asked to use a newspaper or magazine, imagining that she was someone unfamiliar with the events it contained. From what she read, both news articles and advertisements, she was to infer something about life in the United States. She might also pretend to be someone from another planet.

The idea of a visitor from another galaxy gave rise to her wonderfully zany invention of a visiting insect who has come from another solar system with the intention of exploring the planet earth for colonization. Hi creates a character, Xraxis-1227q, Supreme Hive-Queen Commander, who sends telexes back to her Imperial High-Secretary for Defense, Dzreebo-87004884w. She works an ironic twist in the characters themselves: one of the criticisms that the Hive-Queen levels at America is its hostility toward other nations, yet her own planet seems organized along modern lines with a secretary for defense and inhabitants who have social security-like numbers that are extensions of their names. Ha Song Hi also seems to have quite a good time inventing words — the names themselves, "vocorder transcription," "little sisters-under-the-chiton" — which add considerably to the fun and, sometimes, the difficulty of reading the essay. Her technique for determining some of the words is reminiscent of that of the science fiction writer Isaac Asimov, who likes to sit down at a computer and just bang out letters and numbers until he gets a combination that gives rise to an idea or character. Students might enjoy trying that as an aid to invention.

The newspaper becomes the organizing principle for the essay, allowing Hi to take pot shots at whatever event seems to depict life in America. But her point of view is particularly interesting. Since Xraxis is addressing a colleague who shares her language, often words or terms occur without translation. On the other hand, her correspondent — her "nest-sister" — is only partly acquainted with what the Hive-Queen is discussing and must be helped to understand other aspects. This relationship allows the narrator to treat her subject matter in sweeping generalities that sometimes miss the mark quite deliberately. Her parenthetical comments are at once naive and ironic, underscoring the comic effect she achieves with the viewpoint. For example, she seems to confuse the concept of America as an immigrant nation symbolized by a "Golden Door" with the golden arches of McDonald's. She has fun citing *McDonald's: Behind the Arches* as if it were the definitive guide to America.

Nothing escapes the ironic treatment she establishes in the beginning. She contrasts ads for Carnival Cruise Lines with the deprivation of Ethiopian children, making it clear that Americans do not deserve the attention of higher life forms such as may be found on Sol-III. But a problem also develops from the all-inclusive examination, one that students might benefit from discussing. Having established a comic viewpoint, the writer needs to impose a focus that will give more shape to the essay, a point she notes when she reveals that each time she read it "I kept thinking of more to add or change until it finally seemed complete." Using a newspaper as a source, of course, does encourage a global treatment, but learning to select ideas may add significantly to the irony. The note found at the end, which suggests that the invading aliens are ordinary cockroaches, naturally heightens the inherent joke of the essay since we appear to spend a good deal of time eradicating a life force that the writer implies is infinitely more intelligent.

## Further Suggestions for Reading, Writing, and Discussion

Another essay in the text that takes a comic viewpoint is Allison Rolls's "Lady Diana: He Married the Wrong Woman" (page 426), which permits the writer to advance her own cause by assuming a naive stance about her attributes versus those of the Princess of Wales. Writing a proposal to a well-known figure might offer an opportunity for a comedic persuasive essay.

Students might enjoy examining some of the more exotic movie stars or rock singers as if they were an alien life force and the students were scientists who had to make some assumptions and determinations about the culture the stars represent.

## Instructor's Comments: *Constance Kuriyama, Texas Tech University*

I'm inclined to believe that teaching writing must be directed as much as possible to the specific needs of individuals. Most students benefit from three pieces of advice: (1) Write about something you care about but can consider objectively. (2) Try to find a fresh approach to a common topic or seek a more unusual topic. (3) Give careful thought to your audience and how you wish to affect them.

Another technique I have found effective is to give students topics that are relatively flexible and open. As a rule, I give one topic that specifies a writing mode but not a subject, combined with three more "code word" topics tapping a broad area of human experience (such as "using/abusing time," "dreams," "vacations," "a favorite possession"). This helps steer students away from hackneyed topics and stock responses, encouraging them to draw creatively on their experience and observation. Quite often, they will combine the first topic with one of the others to produce interesting results.

## MARK TWAIN, "Letter to the Earth," page 226

### Teaching Strategies

Twain's essay provides an opportunity to discuss how to create a narrator for the purpose of making an argument. The voice we listen to in this essay — the narrator, the "Recording Angel" — is not a developed "character" such as we would see in a short story; he has only enough personality to add force to Twain's criticisms of Andrew Langdon, and hence of American hypocrisy. The narrator even seems to change personality as the essay progresses. At first he seems entirely a minor clerk, obeying orders blindly, mostly concerned with making lists and maintaining accurate balances. His deferential language suggests that he respects Langdon and has no objections to Langdon's horrible prayers being granted. At the end, though, he seems to be speaking ironically when he discusses Langdon's charity and to be "glad" when finally revealing that Langdon is going to hell. The ending might make us question whether the angel was merely adopting a pose in the beginning, but the question is largely irrelevant to the effect of the piece. The character's lack of consistency throughout the piece is less important than the way in which Twain uses the character to make his overall points.

The narrator's "personality" is largely built out of some well-known styles of writing and speaking — the styles of business letters and memos, religious texts and sermons. In the beginning, the angel clerk is all business in style and attitude; in the last two paragraphs religious styles dominate. Twain in essence criticizes business and organized religion by turning their own languages against them. Businessmen are concerned only with how much something is worth in quantifiable monetary terms, so Twain calculates Langdon's moral worth in "carats," as if he were a gem being appraised. Religions teach that what is in a person's heart is more important than what he or she says publicly, so Twain creates a deity that grants the prayers in the man's heart and ignores all his public prayers, including almost everything that happens in churches. Twain thereby suggests that businesses and religions condemn themselves by their own values. Twain uses a dramatic version of the classic device of *reductio ad absurdum* — following someone's arguments until they reach absurd conclusions. Students might practice using Twain's method to criticize other kinds of persons, creating characters who carry the logic of some human pursuit too far — for example, an athlete who wants added muscle might get an operation to have muscles grafted onto his body, with horrifying results.

Almost every line of this essay is ironic; students could study the various ways that Twain undercuts the meaning of his sentences. Some of Twain's methods: understatement (in paragraph 2: "Granted, as follows: diphtheria, 2, 1 fatal"); exaggeration (paragraph 19: "this deed should out-honor all the historic self-sacrifices of men and angels"); contradictions of tone within a sentence (paragraph 8: "I have the honor to call your attention to the fact that you seem to have deteriorated"). Note that the irony gets more heavy-handed as the essay progresses, until near the end Twain is close to outright sarcasm and direct insult (paragraph 17: "Your remaining 401 details count for wind only").

In the beginning of the essay, Twain seems to be mocking the heavenly beings as well as Langdon; his angel seems rather heartless. But by the end, the angels have fairly judged Langdon, and Twain has affixed blame for the horrors in this world not to deities but to humans. It is not clear, however, whether Twain is criticizing all humans or only certain ones. Students might discuss what the world would be like if everyone's secret desires were granted by God. Does any person exist who has not secretly prayed for terrible things?

## Connections to Other Essays

Allison Rolls in "Lady Diana: He Married the Wrong Woman" (page 426) and Alice Kahn in "Pianotherapy: Primal Pop" (page 434) also create personalities for their narrators that are not meant to be taken seriously and that seem to change during the essays. For a discussion of the irony in Rolls's, Kahn's, and Twain's essays, see the instructor's manual entry on Alice Kahn.

"I Forgot the Words to the National Anthem" by James Seilsopour (page 473) also criticizes American hypocrisy from an outsider's point of view. Students might discuss the different ways that Seilsopour and Twain turn their bitterness and anger into effective critical essays.

**WILLIAM G. HILL,** "Returning Home," page 233

## Teaching Strategies

William Hill's essay uses description to render the larger meaning of place. Such an assignment might well begin in the journal with a quick draft of a familiar place from childhood that recalls setting, character, and conversation. Journal drafts should be shared in class, as they may prompt other students to recall similar experiences. Pool halls, candy stores, and soda fountains are frequent subjects for professional writers who wish to re-create not only a setting but a time that has passed.

In his comments about his essay, Hill explains that his purpose for writing the essay shifted from a description of place to an evocation of a period from his childhood that he wanted his readers to understand. Hill's essay does succeed in engaging readers and in making palpable the atmosphere of a small-town pool hall. The essay became a model for description in his class.

Part of what makes "Returning Home" successful is the narrative style. In the laconic voice of the cracker barrel narrator, Hill introduces his subject, lingering over details and personality for the sake of the telling, personalizing descriptions with humorous ease. Hill is adept at sketching, in a few sharp strokes, the characters that populate the "Recreational Club Room." The opening paragraph illustrates Hill's intuitive understanding of how to pull readers into the center of the experience. We see the pool hall much as we might if we walked down the street and encountered the sprawl of checkers players on our own.

Hill capitalizes on the "good old boy" undercurrent of gossip, telling us how things came to pass in the hall but never quite attributing the source of the information. For example, his statements about the sign painter or about Mr. Monroe's prodigious checkers record seem to emanate not so much from the narrator's viewpoint as from his ambition to record the collective wisdom of the loafers and snooker players for whom we imagine no detail is too small to escape comment.

Hill has a sense of the kind of information that readers need. We can easily imagine old man Hall or the tobacco-spitting Democrats chewing away time in the early afternoon. Hill's good pace and sequencing of detail allow us to look about us in leisurely fashion, noting the items in the glass-topped case, inhaling that unique mix of life and "stale smoke, oil from the floor, and, in the winter, fumes from the heater." Students will enjoy the adroit humor in the narrator's voice when he says, "As a rule the boys found a more peaceable way to settle their differences."

With all Hill's talent for description, we regret that he does not tell us more about Possum. Unfortunately, we are left to infer the source of his peace-making might. Possum sounds like the kind of man that small towns create legends about. It might be useful to point out to students the value of expanding characters to dramatize the way of life that is at the heart of a piece.

The theme of the essay, "you can't go home again," verges on the cliché, but not in the hands of a narrator who sidesteps an obvious means to begin his study. Instead Hill leads us to his point and then makes a graceful exit: "I couldn't get very sad about my old hangout not being there anymore; I had left first."

38

## Further Suggestions for Reading, Writing, and Discussion

A number of student essays offer opportunities to test the richness of remembered details: Heather Ashley's "Leaving Vacita" (page 29), Ann Louise Field's "The Sound of Angels" (page 147), An-Thu Quang Nguyen's "Tâi Con" (page 402), and Paula Sisler's "The Water Lily" (page 496).

Students might like to examine excerpts from Thomas Wolfe's *Look Homeward, Angel* to discover the sentiments that prompted Hill's essay.

Students might note the wealth of sensory detail that Eudora Welty evokes in "The Little Store" (page 261) and attempt a similar description. A collection of student memories would make a good classroom publishing project.

## Instructor's Comments: *Sally A. Askew, Northwest Mississippi Junior College, DeSoto Center*

Whenever I discuss the descriptive essay assignment, I always stress that a good description is more than adjectives placed in spatial order, that it should include details and examples which appeal to all the senses if possible. The students can usually manage this much, if only by forcing themselves. They must also, of course, have a point to make with the description, even if the point is an implied one. This part of the assignment is usually more difficult for them. Williams's paper is successful because it sounds so natural that it doesn't reek of the requirements. It stands out, quite simply, because it doesn't read like an assignment.

I used this essay as a model for a description in later classes. We discussed its strengths and the reasons it was effective. One student pointed out that after reading it, she actually felt a sense of loss because the place was gone, though she had never actually been anywhere near it.

I really think the only way to get students to write well is to let them have plenty of time to perfect their work. The way I teach is mostly a rebellion against the way I was taught. I was given fifty minutes to choose a subject, write the paper, and proofread it, and I was never encouraged at all. I am sure that the lack of encouragement must have been because my papers were more frantic than inspired. In-class assignments test only one kind of ability. Students need to be able to brood over their subjects. Besides, after I tell them to organize and proofread so meticulously and choose every word so carefully, it would be rather ludicrous to expect miracles in fifty minutes.

## EUDORA WELTY, "The Little Store," page 239

### Teaching Strategies

Eudora Welty plays with time in her essay. The opening is in the past tense, a narrator recalling her childhood. However, for most of the story of a trip to the Little Store, she attaches the auxiliary *would* or *might* to the verbs, putting us in a strange time that is not precisely present or past. In paragraph 4, when the narrator says "I would" in response to the question "Who'd like to run to the Little Store for me?," it is both the present, adult narrator and the writer as a child who are saying "I would."

Welty uses some other unusual devices to blur the borders between present and past. In paragraph 13 she switches from first- to second-person point of view, from describing what "I" did to describing what "you met" when "you" went into the store. This device serves to generalize her experience, to make her experience that of a whole generation. In paragraph 15, she switches to the present tense. In paragraph 16 she once again uses *might* and *would* as well as the past tense. In paragraphs 18–19 she brings back "I" but mixes in some uses of "you." These shifts of person and verb form serve to destroy the barrier of time and the distinction between the person she is now and the one she was then. If "you can" go to the store now, then the narrator has not lost the store or the person she used to be.

Occasionally, Welty switches to a fully adult voice, dropping all pretense of imagining herself back at the store. In paragraphs 11, 26, and 27 she describes the effect of her surroundings on the child she was. The environment and the people around her became "indelible" impressions and "stories" that exist in that indeterminate time of fiction and memories. This essay re-creates the world of memory, not the world of childhood, and all the strange shifts of person and verb form mirror the strange eternal present in which memories exist.

Welty's use of the *would* and *might* verb forms creates that "eternal present": by speaking of what "would" happen when her mother "would" send her to the store, the narrator avoids speaking of specific real events and talks instead of likely events, typical events, of the general nature of experience, not of distinct experiences. Occasionally she does mention something that happened on a particular day, such as her parade on the first Armistice Day, and then she drops into the past tense. But these specific memories merely punctuate her generalized tale of the sort of things that happened all the time.

Welty draws us into an unchanging world in which every event "could" occur again. She re-creates the stable, secure, eternal world of childhood, just as William Hill does, and she too leads up to the mysterious moment when this world disappeared, when the people who ran the Little Store moved away. Unlike Hill, she has some idea how the change occurred — through some act of violence — but the vague fact explains little. All she finally can say is that "the story broke off." She seems sad that she has lost her safe childhood haven, but she also lets us know that all during her childhood she was "on the track" of the "human mystery" that includes death and violence. She sought, as all children seek, the end of childhood, the end of the sweet, secure haven the store had been. She wanted that story to be broken off. Her essay also breaks off abruptly. Imaginary, unchanging worlds cannot end in an easy way; they stop abruptly when something interrupts them, usually the demands of reality.

**Connections to Other Essays**

Many of the essays in this collection present radically different views of childhood. Some of the writers view childhood as Eudora Welty does — a time of sweet innocence whose loss is to be mourned ("Leaving Vacita" by Heather Ashley [page 29], "Once More to the Lake" by E. B. White [page 39], "Returning Home" by William G. Hill [page 233]). James Baldwin's "Notes of a Native Son" (page 156), Joan Didion's "On Going Home" (page 255), Maxine Hong Kingston's "The Woman Warrior" (page 417), Christopher Nolan's "Knife Used" (page 461) provide some balance to this view, showing some of the pains and limitations of childhood and some of the reasons why children want to grow up and break out of their families. John Clyde Thatcher's "On Killing the Man" (page 515), Doris Lessing's "Old Chief Mshlanga (page 522), and James Joyce's "Araby" (page 507) show how the wonderful idealizations and illusions of childhood sometimes can *cause* pains. Richard Rodriguez in "Hunger and Memory" (page 478) presents his childhood among his family as a warm, intimate period from which he was forced by his desire to succeed. He feels the loss but believes it is a loss that everyone must accept to succeed in the public world.

**JUDY JENNINGS,** "Second-Class Mom," page 248

**Teaching Strategies**

Judy Jennings's essay was written in response to an assignment on explanation: "Explain a person, event, situation in life you understand very well to an audience who needs or wants to know more about the subject. Instead of teaching your audience how to do something, in this paper you will tell them *what* your subject is all about."

The assignment itself was helpful because it specified an audience — imagine a real publication as the recipient — thus helping the writer to shape the information to suit the needs of a particular audience. Explanatory papers are a staple of composition courses, but Jennings's essay shows that even this most traditional task allows students to explore personal topics. Jennings might just as easily have used a narrative to explain her point: indeed, while the essay contains elements of narrative, it fulfills the more specific guidelines set down by an explanatory assignment. Jennings's ability to generalize about a subjective experience makes the essay successful.

Many readers of this essay will undoubtedly be grateful to Jennings for tackling the subject. Jennings's instructor, Rica Garcia, notes, "As both a parent and a stepparent, I realized immediately I was in Judy's audience, and I caught myself smiling and nodding with a kind of relief as I read her words which somehow validated my own experience as a stepmother." Jennings tells us that her purpose was "to clarify a misunderstood role." She envisioned as an audience the readers of *Growing Parent Magazine,* a publication that might easily include such subject matter.

The essay gives enough background to allow the reader to sympathize with the writer's point of view. The central point she makes — the disparity between what is expected emotionally of stepparents and what are the emotional realities of such a role — is rendered dispassionately. Jennings never sidesteps the unpleasant details, nor does she cast herself in a light that makes her seem noble. All the uncertainties, the hidden messages, the jealousies that are attendant in remarriage are given voice: " 'Your husband used to be in love with someone else,' and some things are better left unthought."

Her ability to move from the personal to the general also gives the essay substance. She understands the larger issue — that of all the parenting roles society casts upon us, the complexities of being a stepparent may be the most misunderstood and unappreciated. Paragraph 6 contains an example of how Jennings reaches beyond her immediate situation to the larger reality of her audience. She asks readers to see the role not only in its own circumstance but in comparison to any of the other roles we may choose for ourselves as parents. And this is exactly her thesis — the absence of choice. Some students in the class who are themselves stepchildren may wish to argue this point. There is no doubt that the essay will provoke heated debates, but you may want to remind the class that the issue is not whether one point of view or the other is valid — the point is that the writer has tackled an almost unspoken subject with candor and in doing so should find a receptive audience for her courage and skill in handling an unpopular issue.

**Further Suggestions for Reading, Writing, and Discussion**

Fairy tales, which are a main source of portraits of stepmothers, reflect wide cultural assumptions about the disruption that occurs to families when a remarriage takes place. It might be interesting to have students read "Cinderella" and "Hansel and Gretel" again, asking them to note how each role is defined — that of the children, Hansel, Gretel, Cinderella; that of the two fathers; that of the stepsisters; that of the stepmothers. A class discussion might center on the stereotypes that surround these roles and what emotional claims, what property rights, are affected by a new family structure.

If possible, it would be interesting to have students bring in different versions of the two stories, particularly illustrated tales, where the stereotypes are reinforced even more clearly by the pictures.

Students might enjoy writing a modern fairy tale in which they explore some stereotype or role with which they are familiar. For example, a story of a good child and a bad child, a person who undergoes a change, a task set by someone wicked that sets a loved one free — all the staples of fairy tale lore reflect some deeper universal assumptions about the nature of relationships. Ask students to list their favorite tales and select a few that might be read out loud. Then have them rewrite a tale using their own characters and settings, but be sure to have them draw some larger point by the telling.

## Instructor's comments: *Rica Garcia, Richland College*

My advice to students: Writing is a recursive process. Go through all the stages of inventing, shaping, completing, and back again. Writing is like baking bread. It's never easy and you can't rush the process, but after the first few times you know the bread will turn out if you just go through the process.

Save editing for the last draft of the writing process. Be willing to revise, change your whole article, write, and rewrite. When you are finally satisfied, then you can edit. (That nasty voice in your head that loves to criticize your work should really be useful in looking up misspelled words, checking commas, typing, etc. It's just her kind of thing.)

Get at least three or four readers for your drafts. Have classmates read your work and give you their opinions. You can't tell whether a piece works unless you let others read it.

Write to give value to a specific audience. Invent the audience carefully and get to know them well before you begin to write a draft. Imagine a person within that audience and then write with him or her specifically in mind.

Write in your own voice, not the one you think your ninth-grade English teacher would like.

Tell the voice in your head that says, "You can't write . . . this is stupid . . . you better not put this down on paper or someone might see it . . . you better write only about pleasant things," to leave you alone. Don't let your ability to write now be governed by voices from the past saying that you can't write. The critical voices in your head probably know very little about writing anyway.

Forget about perfection. If you like to be 100 percent right all the time, you'll play it safe as a writer. Some people never write anything (from letters to dissertations) because they are afraid it won't be perfect. You have to give yourself permission to mess up if you are going to be a writer.

Read. Not to copy others' styles but to learn to recognize voice and style and to learn how to use the English language.

Keep a journal. Write down ideas for articles; write when you are miserable; write when something special happens; write why you're trying to figure your life out; write so you can make meaning of your thoughts.

Write with publication in mind. You won't have to publish, but forget about writing to the English teacher. You are a person writing articles for possible publication, not an English student writing essays for an instructor.

My advice to instructors: I have my students keep a journal. However, I regard journals as private writing, and students cannot use them as such if they think someone is going to read them. I know many entries in my journal would be ripped out at the mere thought of some English teacher poring over my private life. Consequently, I now require the Private Journal. It must be 50 pages long (250 words = 1 page) with date entries spaced throughout the semester. I glance at the journal to be sure it is a journal, entries are written at proper intervals, and then just count the pages and given an automatic A (90–100) for completion of the assignment. I save the 100s for the students who write much more than 50 pages, as several always do. The journal counts 10 percent of the course grade.

Students must have three classmates read their drafts and fill out what I call a Reader's Sheet. Each assignment has a different set of questions depending on what skill is being introduced or stressed in that article (detail, audience, thesis). Furthermore, the writers are urged to have one member of their "real" audience read the piece. I also require that writers read aloud their work to at least one person so they can both hear the words and watch for nonverbal reactions.

I often think the readers get more out of this collaboration than the writers, but I'm convinced it is a valuable activity for all involved. The writers begin to get over their fear of being read, get feedback, and form a writing peer group which offers encouragement and support as well as advice; the readers get to analyze the writing of others. All learn.

**JOAN DIDION,** "On Going Home," page 255

**Teaching Strategies**

Joan Didion's realistic tone is created by a kind of constant undercutting of what she says. She does not believe that any part of life can be accurately described in any single view, so she goes back and forth, first making something seem terrible, then revealing good parts of it, then qualifying how good it is. For example, in her first paragraph she describes discussions at her parents' house as quite cold and even cruel; these people either talk about real estate or gossip about who has been committed to mental hospitals. But then she says that her family is actually "talking in code" about pleasant things, about "yellow fields and the cottonwoods and the rivers rising and falling." Similarly, she ends the first paragraph saying, "Marriage is the classic betrayal." We are prepared for further scenes of marital tensions, but she immediately retracts her generalization: "Or perhaps it is not anymore."

Didion focuses almost entirely on ugly details. Nobody is sweet or kind; no room is beautiful. When she drives into the country, it is to visit a graveyard — and even the graveyard is ugly, having been vandalized. But Didion is not telling us about how terrible her life is, because we can tell that she derives a peculiar pleasure from these ugly details, and she brings us to appreciate them as well. She clearly loves her husband, even though she says little nice about him and seems to battle with him constantly, and we can see how such a love, not blinded to flaws, could be stronger than a love that casts the loved one as some kind of ideal.

Didion's essay is about two types of families — the type she grew up in (a "home") and the type she now is a part of (somehow not a "home"). At first we might try to decide which kind she prefers. Eventually we realize that she is not trying to choose; she is presenting the flaws and the joys of both. This essay is not about how terrible families used to be or about how terrible they are becoming. Rather, she is documenting a change from one kind of family to another, and she is utterly ambivalent about both kinds.

43

In old families, people neurotically invested all their emotions, expecting to find in "home" all the meaning of life. In such homes, emotional relations became guerrilla wars — "wars" because people were repeatedly cruel to each other, "guerrilla" because the cruelty was hidden in the illusion of Home Sweet Home. But at least there were strong ties; people had an emotional center, even if they ended up carrying that center about with them long after it served any purpose. Nowadays, Didion says, "home" has no such emotional weight. The net result is partly a loss of caring, as shown in the scene of a young girl on drugs performing striptease. The girl does not inspire thoughts of romantic degradation because there is no sense that she has thrown away "home"; she has no innocence to strip off because she was never covered in the false white dress that "home" casts over young girls. There is no great evil in what the girl is doing because there is no great purity or goodness to destroy.

The loss of "home" has some benefits as well: it gives people freedom from useless emotional baggage. What children take with them from their families are much "lighter," more pleasant things, as Didion indicates in the last line. Instead of photographs and hand-painted teacups full of the past, burdening young women, especially, with the need to live for family, Didion's daughter will "inherit" a xylophone, a "sundress from Madeira," and a "funny story." This new collection of treasures will not weigh her down — she will be able to make music, run, and laugh, rather than brooding about what she should feel about her family.

Few writers can balance praise and blame, joy and pain as carefully as Didion can. Few writers can convey ambivalence about everything without having their writing dissolve into shapeless ambiguity. Consider, for example, the little symbolic scene of the "family graveyard." The symbolism might seem simple at first: this is a place where "family" has been buried. But more important is the fact that the graveyard has been vandalized, the monuments broken. What the scene shows is the loss of emotional ties to the dead; to the vandals, the monuments did not carry intense associations. The vandals were not indulging in satanic rituals; they were not desecrating. They were probably just young folks on drugs, stripping off the "clothing" of the dead, very much like the young girl Didion described earlier. Didion is partly appalled and partly happy that the graveyard is vandalized; something mysterious and romantic has been destroyed, but at the same time people have been freed of the necessity of paying homage to and taking care of the dead.

## Connections to Other Essays

Didion's essay provides a set of terms for analyzing family relationships that could be applied to the other essays about families in this collection, such as "The Sound of Angels" by Ann Louise Field (page 147), "Notes of a Native Son" by James Baldwin (page 156), "The Woman Warrier" by Maxine Hong Kingston (page 417), and "The Little Store" by Eudora Welty (page 239). To apply Didion's terms, consider these questions: Do family members speak in "code"? Are there "ambushes"? Is there a "guerrilla war" going on? Do children feel a "nameless anxiety" when they grow up and leave the family? Field and Welty, in the beginning of their essays, seem to show families whose members do not ambush each other, but by the end rather dark secrets are revealed that destroy the illusion of Home Sweet Home. Kingston and Baldwin show families whose daily lives are full of ambushes, but, like Didion, they do not simply throw away "family"; they try to negotiate the minefields to extract what is still of value. Students might discuss why no writers seem to portray fully happy families. Do they never exist, or are they too dull to write about?

**EARNESTINE JOHNSON,** "Thank You Miss Alice Walker: *The Color Purple*," page 259

## Teaching Strategies

The assignment that gave rise to Johnson's essay was based on a journal entry that students had been asked to do in response to a reading assignment. The journal took the form of a learning or reading log with the following instructions: "You are asked to keep a journal in which you respond to what you have read a minimum of twice a week and at least fifteen minutes per entry. Your responses may focus on a character, the tone, a value you share or don't share, a point that was unclear; or your response may be experimental — a short story or poem of your own, a parody, a dialogue. The focus is up to you. Your main concerns are dealing with the material and generating ideas. Don't be afraid to follow an impulse, argue with the author, or puzzle over the ending."

The concept of the reading log is significant for helping to break through students' seeming passivity in approaching both written assignments and class discussion of a reading. At the heart of the idea is the invitation to students to become active interrogators of the text. Generally the questions that develop out of the log entries are of a high order. Too often students are reluctant to ask questions or express an opinion during class meetings, fearing that their ideas lack substance. The reading log offers them an opportunity to generate rather than simply respond to questions. The log, as given in the assignment, offers students a wide variety of choices — argue, question, re-create, parody, invent — so that they are not committed to examining a text from one point of view. This is a rich learning opportunity that is likely to help even the most diffident or shy student. However, one note of caution: having given the invitation, instructors must be prepared to be open to the ways in which students respond because the heart of the idea is trust — trust that all ideas or responses have equal weight. Once the trust is established, discussions soon become lively forums for competing ideas and understanding.

Johnson's essay offers an interesting insight into how the process works. At first she was reluctant to deal with the text: "I read the first page and closed the book. I was ashamed of the ignorant definitions given to the parts of the body. I was embarrassed by the explicitness of the sex act. I opened and closed the book many times before I could go beyond the first page." From this initial point, the essay becomes a reflection of the complex nature of the reader-writer relationship. It takes the form of a direct address to the author, a one-sided conversation in which the writer brings together her experiences, both past and present, with that of the central character of the Walker novel. We have a sense of someone talking out loud to another writer, to herself, to the people in her class, to her mother, and to the events of her childhood. The essay allows us as readers to watch Johnson both as reader and writer, talking, arguing her way through the experience. What we discover is a student who is taking charge of her learning.

Johnson is responding to several audiences. Her anger is directed first at Walker, who has seemingly embarrassed her. She is also angry at her classmates' naiveté. But perhaps she is angriest at herself for denying the truth of the experience that she has repressed: "Why, of all the subjects to write about, do you choose one which hurts me so deeply? I am furious with you." The challenge to Walker provides Johnson with an opportunity to call up her own memories and to present them side by side with Celie and Shug Avery. Here Johnson becomes the writer, the inventor of her own world and the characters who people it: Mrs. Brown, Mama Liz. Almost effortlessly, Johnson shifts back and forth between her responses to the text and the evocation of her past. From Walker's characters she infers the lessons that she had to learn; from the dialogue she has caught "memories of faces and voices that had long ceased to exist."

It is not necessary to have read the novel to understand Johnson's response. Preeminently what the reader learns is how the writer feels about the text, not precisely what happened. This is one of the values of the reading log. The focus is on the reader's interpretation of the text: it is admittedly biased in favor of the reader initially. By allowing for the emotional scope of Johnson's response, the assignment prompted a significant lesson in which the student made connections between her own experience and that of the author. We cannot ask for much more.

## Further Suggestions for Reading, Writing, and Discussion

Other student essays that deal with the reading process and student interpretation of another text are those by Judy Benson and Amber Kennish in *Student Writers at Work,* second edition, and Margot Harrison's "Creative Transfiguration from the Death of a Moth" (page 201).

One way to distinguish a log from a journal is to think of the journal as a more private piece of writing, something that will be read only by the writer or perhaps an instructor. A log is a more public instrument — it is the record of a shared experience not unlike a ship's log or an airplane pilot's log. In the class it is a record of the learning of a shared text or task.

Students may enjoy keeping a reading log. Assign some reading, a short story, a poem, or a short essay. Ask them to imagine that they have an opportunity to discuss the text with the writer, to raise questions, to point out omissions, to add anything they think will clarify the reading. Point out that these logs will be shared either in small discussion groups or in whole-class discussions. You might also ask them as a result of their entries to generate some questions or topics they would like to address in a written assignment. One point must be made: do not expect students to generate wonderful assignments immediately. Having "received" assignments as a matter of course over the many years of their education, they are likely to be intimidated by the freedom to choose. You might assign several log entries before allowing students to try their own hand at an assignment. Give them some leisure to reflect or speculate first.

Another way to involve reading logs in class activities is to have students take fifteen minutes during a discussion to write down their reactions or questions to a controversial point and then ask them to read their reactions out loud. The more the students are thrown back on their own resources, the more likely we are to get the vigorous kinds of discussions we all hope for.

## Instructor's Comments: *Lois Cucullu, George Mason University*

I was struck by the honesty, the intensity, and the change Earnestine underwent in her essay. In reading it, I felt her experience paralleled that of Celie (the main character in the novel) in her frustration to express herself openly. Similarly, Earnestine was able to come to terms with her past, in the process of responding to the novel, and value her present self. Her insights about Walker's characters, moreover, aided my appreciation of the work. In short, her essay enhanced my understanding of the novel and the truth of human relationships.

My usual procedure with class work is to display it informally on the bulletin board in the classroom. This gives class members an opportunity to read it, honors the authors, and becomes a resource for the class.

I should also add that with each new class, I begin the term displaying past student work. Earnestine's essay and drafts have been used in this way. Since my different classes meet in this room, these works (including Earnestine's) have a wider audience than my one class.

To improve their writing, students need help becoming readers of their own work. This is in essence what revision means. They also need to realize that revision is not easy. It requires patience, thought, and distance.

I have thought a lot about this, and, while I am certain that my ideas are not original, I believe it comes down to one word — audience. By audience I mean that learning takes place when students have a sense that a subject or a work is addressed to them, that they *are its audience;* consequently, their opinions, thoughts, and insights, matter, i.e., they in turn *have an audience* When they perceive themselves in this way, learning results and the results are no less than remarkable.

**ALICE WALKER,** "A Letter of the Times, or Should This Sado-Masochism Be Saved?" page 266

## Teaching Strategies

Alice Walker's essay shows how a writer can modulate the distance between herself and her readers. Since sadomasochism is an exotic subject for most people, the title suggests that this essay will be about things unrelated to most of our lives. The first paragraph, in contrast, gives us the sense of overhearing an intimate conversation between friends, making us feel the essay is about the most familiar of subjects — friends' relations to each other. Throughout the essay, Walker moves back and forth, creating distance with talk of lesbians and slavery, then bringing us close with talk of what is in everyone's hearts. Finally, she brings her exotic subjects and her familiar style together in the discussion of a woman dressing up as Scarlett O'Hara. We can easily imagine dressing as Scarlett — or as Rhett Butler — but we have rarely thought about what our admiration for such slave owners means. Walker makes us think that some of our actions may be comparable to sadomasochism or slavery, things we thought unrelated to our lives.

In this essay, Walker seeks to make us have the experience that Susan Marie tries to give her class — to make us "unable . . . to think of enslaved women as exotic, picturesque, removed from themselves, deserving of enslavement." In other words, Walker seeks to remove the distance that we set between ourselves and enslaved women. Susan Marie is closer to enslaved women than we are, and Lucy is closer to Susan Marie than we are, so the characters in this essay serve as bridges to carry us across the distance separating us from "enslaved women."

The second-person point of view is well suited for manipulating the distance between reader and narrator. We feel at times that the narrator is addressing us when she says "you," and at other times we separate ourselves and say, "This speaker is talking to that other person." Walker takes advantage of these two relations that readers might have to the voice in the essay. The questions in this essay can be divided into those that are addressed only to Lucy (such as "Do you remember the things I told you about the class?" in paragraph 4) and those that seem addressed to us as well as to Lucy (such as "Does anyone want to be a slave?" in paragraph 16 or "What do you think?" in the last paragraph). We can easily feel that we are in the same position in relation to Susan Marie's philosophy that Lucy is — we simply had never thought about these issues in this way before. Our thoughtless admiration of the main characters in *Gone With the Wind* makes us very much like Lucy, and we can imagine Susan Marie snubbing us for expressing that admiration.

The relationship between Lucy and Susan Marie also shifts in "distance" during the essay. The opening paragraph tells us of a rift between the two, and the ending shows that some of this rift has been healed ("you and I will be friends again"). It is precisely by gaining an understanding of the large issues that Susan Marie discusses that Lucy will become a friend again. Similarly, we can become "friends" with Alice Walker by gaining an understanding of the points she makes in this essay. However, if we disagree with the essay, we are essentially maintaining our distance from Walker.

Students might note the freedom of organization that the letter format allows. In a letter, side issues can be brought in and dropped easily; a writer can say, "I will get on to the point," as Walker does in the middle. When students find themselves confused about how to organize a formal essay, they might try writing their ideas in a letter to an imaginary friend. By doing so, they might discover a way to organize their ideas into a formal essay, or they might decide that leaving the essay in letter format works well.

Walker's essay does have an overall structure; it starts and ends with "personal issues" — the snub — and puts all the abstract talk about slavery and God in the middle. This structure helps Walker's argument that our personal lives have important issues at their center. We cannot separate what is personal and what is impersonal or seemingly irrelevant to our lives — our personal lives are bound up with (or surround) large, abstract issues.

An interesting feature of Walker's argument is her pitting of feminists (who might admire Scarlett for her independence) and civil rights activists against each other. We often tend to lump left-wing movements together, whether we favor them or not.

## Connections to Other Essays

Several other essays in this collection use the second-person point of view. Ha Song Hi's "From Xraxis to Dzreebo" (page 216) and Mark Twain's "Letter to the Earth" (page 226) both use the letter format as Alice Walker does. Jo Goodwin Parker's "What Is Poverty?" (page 555) is written as a dramatic monologue to a person who resists the writer's argument. These essays show particularly clearly how a writer creates both his or her own voice (and hence a writing personality) and an implied audience. After studying the kind of personas these authors create for themselves and their audiences, students can analyze the more subtly created narrators and implied audiences of essays written in the third or first person.

In "Tools of Torture," Phyllis Rose (page 543) argues that the wearing of symbols of slavery and torture (such as spiked bracelets) is a good sign; she believes that it is good to treat such issues lightly and playfully. Rose would presumably approve of dressing up as Scarlett O'Hara. Rose and Walker clearly disagree, and students could debate the two views. Rose's essay makes a nice match to Walker's because it also brings together the familiar, everyday world of fashion and the fairly distant world of politics. These two essays show two ways of mixing personal experience and abstract topics.

"Sojourner Truth: And A'n't I a Woman?" by Frances Dana Barker Gage (page 315) addresses both feminism and slavery as Walker does. Students might discuss the ways these issues have changed (or have not changed) in the last hundred years.

**DIANE KOCOUR,** "The Diet Industry Knows Best — Or Does It?," page 272

## Teaching Strategies

In her student questionnaire, Kocour addresses the issue of the writer's personal involvement in a topic:

Ironically, the idea of writing on the diet industry was one that I wasn't quite sure about in the beginning. I was asked to select a topic for a documented argumentative essay which would be interesting, controversial, factual, and above all, one which I had strong opinions on or some type of background in. When ideas began to surface, I had difficulty finding one with which I was completely comfortable. . . . The idea of writing on the challenges I was facing at the time was always in the back of my mind. These challenges involved battling a compulsive eating disorder that brought me dangerously close to bulimia.

Initially, however, I wasn't quite sure of how to put something so emotional into a category that could be factual and argumentative. This question was answered when I took the time to sit down and assess what exactly it was that had gotten me into such a dangerous situation. After examining myself and my past for some time, it became clear to me that I was just one of the many who had become obsessed with an industry that promised quick and effective results and imprisoned helpless people to lives of food dependency and self-blame. I realized that I held within myself tremendous anger for this industry and also realized that it could be a subject which would be capable of being researched and reported on. I had stumbled on a topic that satisfied all the [course] requirements, and one which I could hardly wait to begin researching.

Kocour's very full explanation of her commitment to her subject offers the student a compelling statement of the struggle a writer undergoes in trying to balance interest with objectivity. But unlike Curtis Chang, who declares his connection to his research topic (in "Streets of Gold," page 90) Kocour decides not to reveal her own quest to lose weight. Although the tone is impassioned, the impressive information she uses to prove her point never once wavers from a clearly third-person, objective stance.

The essay begins with an illustration of a supermarket customer who at the very moment she is buying food is being reminded of her weight. Students should note the value of selecting a telling illustration to begin the attack. It allows the writer to get to the heart of the controversy economically and persuasively. Reader identification with the issue is clear: we are that customer; we know those products; we have listened to those commercials; we have read those ads. A brief historical overview lends further strength to the underlying generalization of the essay, which appears first in paragraph 3: "It is this obsession to be thin that completely imprisons people, making them victims of an industry that capitalizes on the impatience and nutritional ignorance of people who are in search of the perfect body at the same time that it claims to be helping them."

By the time the generalization has been introduced, Kocour has accomplished an initial goal for the essay, "an earnest appeal to the emotions of my readers." Kocour brings an impressive array of opinion to the subject. Citing psychological studies and marketing research, she covers a wide range of diets, diet programs, and diet products that interest consumers. Students should also note how successfully she introduces each expert or study, allowing readers to understand in a clear and economical way the source of information without having to turn to endnotes. The steady piling up of information is interrupted briefly in paragraph 11 when Kocour invites readers directly to do some reflecting: "Stop and think about that for a moment." Coming as it does after so much information, it is a welcome opportunity for readers to share directly in the argument. It also provides a halfway point for the attack. Whereas the first part of the essay focuses on the background and widespread interests of the diet industry, the second half details the chicanery and deception being practiced. By the time Kocour reaches her conclusion, readers are prepared for the force of the denunciation.

(text pages 286–292)

The paragraph structure in the essay deserves attention. You might ask students to look at the way the paragraphs appear, without any attention initially to content. What they might notice is the evenness of the paragraphs, which on the surface suggests some real control. Then ask students to look at their own papers. Are the paragraphs even in length, or are some quite short and others very long? While there is no magic rule for creating paragraphs, generally in an argument the appearance of many short paragraphs indicates a problem in organization. Class time might be spent examining coherence and structure and how it is achieved.

## Further Suggestions for Reading, Writing, and Discussion

Students might compare several argument papers using the strategy for a descriptive outline suggested in this manual under the discussion of Bonnie Harris's "The Healing Power of Music" (p. 176).

## Instructor's Comments: *Marvin Diogenes, University of Arizona*

Learn to take your time when writing. Good essays (or stories or poems) take a long time to write. The semester is an arbitrary, artificial unit of time. If you're serious about writing, the pieces you begin now will stay with you, evolve, improve. You'll come back to them later in life.

## THOMAS JEFFERSON, "The Declaration of Independence," page 286

### Teaching Strategies

The Declaration of Independence is difficult to see as a piece of writing because of its tremendous importance in our history. The grand principles that begin the document have such a familiar ring that it is hard to imagine anyone thinking them up. To help students see the process that resulted in this document, have them imagine the kind of controversies that would lead a group of persons to decide to overthrow a government. It should become apparent that the motivating force behind revolution has to be anger at the injustice of the government; therefore, the authors of the Declaration probably began with the list of abuses in the middle and then added as an introduction the abstract principles of the first two paragraphs. Students can probably imagine people actually writing the list of abuses; we can see genuine human passion, with all its biases and flawed thinking, in them.

To bring students to see the passion in the list of abuses, consider these strongly charged passages:

1. In paragraph 15, Jefferson says the king has sent "swarms of Officers to harass our People, and eat out their substance." The word "swarms" suggests that the officers are insects, not humans — who descend like a plague of supernatural locusts and "eat out" everything, even human substance.

2. In paragraph 29, "He has plundered our seas, ravaged our Coasts, burnt our towns, and destroyed the Lives of our people." Before this passage, Jefferson sounds like a lawyer making charges against a citizen in court; this passage turns to outright attack. It also is neatly constructed, its series of parallel phrases building to a climax, as each one gets closer to home — from sea to coast to town to people's lives. In this sentence we see the king traveling from England, destroying everything in his path.

3. Paragraph 30 in its entirety, especially the phrase "Cruelty & Perfidy scarcely paralleled in the most barbarous ages," seems quite a large claim given the kind of stories told in the eighteenth century about "barbarous ages" when Christians were slaughtered in grotesque ways by heathens.

4. In paragraph 32, which ends the list of abuses, students might be surprised that the last, and apparently the worst, crime of the king is that he enlisted the "Indian Savages" to fight for him. Since the colonists are trying to prove that the king deserves to be condemned by the basic principles of civilized men everywhere, it is important to claim that the king is in league with those outside European civilization. The Indians are described as fighting in an inhuman way, killing women, children, and sick people — "undistinguished destruction of all ages, sexes and conditions." Colonists did in fact know of peaceful Indians, so this passage is a blatant appeal to the prejudices of most Europeans. Helping students to recognize that this document has such flaws might allow them to see it as an essay like the others in this course. Jefferson, with all his political genius, was limited by the views and prejudices of his age.

The passion in these passages is carefully balanced by the rest of the Declaration. The colonists do not simply want a shrill, violent document; they want to appear calm, reasonable people facing a barbarous, irrational king (hoping to take advantage of King George III's reputation as almost insane and one of the worst kings in British history). They thus surround their angry accusations with characterizations of themselves. Within the list of abuses, the colonists speak of the laws they want as "the most wholesome" (paragraph 6), of their protesting with "manly firmness" (paragraph 10), and of petitioning "in the most humble terms" (paragraph 33). The colonists make themselves seem decent, wholesome, patient, humble, and manly. "Manly" means that the revolutionaries were not skulking around, sabotaging the government in a devious way. However, it might be interesting to discuss why masculinity would be important to mention in this document (the king is often referred to as being father to his people, which makes the people inferior, as children and wives were; the colonists, by rebelling, are in a sense seeking to assume the role of the adult male, the father).

The opening and closing paragraphs show most clearly how the colonists want to characterize themselves. These paragraphs are written from a grand, serene perspective, suggesting that the authors of this document are not petty, vindictive persons, but men of wide vision. The opening paragraphs are full of phrases that go beyond politics or law to use the language of abstract philosophy and religion. The first five paragraphs form a classic "funnel" introduction to an essay, starting with phrases applying to everything ("the Laws of Nature and Nature's God"), moving to "all men," then to "Governments," and finally to the "King of Great Britain." The last sentence of the Declaration returns to "Divine Providence" and pledges of "sacred honor," moving once again outside the specifically political focus of the document. The Declaration is based on the philosophical assumption that individuals stand outside and can judge governments, and its structure reflects this belief, surrounding specific talk of governments with talk about rights and pledges of individuals.

The Declaration is often discussed as an example of deductive argument, setting up general principles, relating particular cases to those principles, and then drawing conclusions. The whole essay takes the form of a syllogism. But it still requires passion and charged language to make this logical argument work. To see why logic needs the support of passion, students might consider whether the king would have accepted either the general principles of the beginning or the list of "Facts . . . submitted to a candid world."

**Connections to Other Essays**

The Declaration relies on many of the verbal devices that Aldous Huxley condemns in "Words and Behavior" (page 103). Jefferson relies heavily on abstractions and personifies the British nation, treating everything the British have done as the acts of one man, the king. Students might try rewriting parts of the Declaration to eliminate the "linguistic errors" that Huxley decries.

**KAREN L. KRAMER,** "The Little Drummer Boys," page 292

**Teaching Strategies**

Karen Kramer's assignment was to write a traditional comparison and contrast essay. Her response is proof that students can write this kind of essay and have a wonderful time doing it. As she puts it, "The goal of my essay was to have fun, pure and simple. No earth-shattering messages here."

From the start, she establishes a working relationship with her audience much in the manner of Matthew Holicek (*Student Writers at Work,* second edition), who also seems to be enjoying his classification of horror movies and is certain that his readers will share in his pleasure. Kramer begins her lively challenge to her audience in her opening sentence when she invites them to join in making distinctions between drummers and percussionists: "Quick — what do you call a person who plays the trumpet?" From that point on, she engages her readers directly in the debate, frequently firing questions or asking for participation much in the manner of a stage emcee.

But the essay is not just a breezy monologue, Kramer has made a real study of the differences and created a character for each type, contrasting the "rabid, primordial Neanderthal" drummer's appeal to the masses with the nonsmoking, nondrinking, conservative "Oral Roberts" percussionists's more sedate performance. She extends the comparison well beyond the types themselves, explaining the different ways that conductors react to them, distinctions that exist between their techniques, their use of instruments, even their feelings about their instruments. This is where Kramer really seems to be having a splendid time, taking pokes at both groups and assuming that her readers will share her enthusiasm.

Students should note the complex interconnections that she establishes and that free the essay from the formulaic conventions that comparison and contrast assignments so often follow. Paragraph 8 offers a good example of how Kramer avoids listing differences; instead, she uses a series of conditional clauses to draw her contrasts: "Whereas the drummer is merely interested in creating as much noise as possible, music . . . is of importance to the percussionist. Whether it be a well-placed cymbal crash or a tiny 'ting' on the triangle, the percussionist, with utmost precision, makes the most of it without overpowering the ensemble with which he happens to be playing. . . . Percussionists, who are able to create the sound illusion of a trotting horse or a babbling brook, are as subtle as a morning breezed blowing across the dew-covered grass, whereas drummers, who do their best to create the illusion of an artillery barrage, are about as subtle as a panzer division smashing through the concert hall."

Also giving vitality to the essay is Kramer's obvious expertise on the subject. This is a point that cannot be repeated too often. If students have an opportunity to write on a topic about which they have real knowledge, even the most traditional assignment becomes a lively forum for their experience. It is clear that Kramer, like Holicek, is a natural observer. The essay is loaded with detail, from which she extrapolates further comparisons. Note paragraph 3, where she takes sideswipes at percussionists by inference while she describes the ways in which drummers attack their equipment: "Cymbals do not ever come in pairs, except for the high hat. Triangles, sleigh bells, woodblocks, etc., are for second-grade rhythm bands, not drummers. As for kettle drums, as far as the drummer is concerned, they're used for boiling water. The xylophone is merely a word in an A-B-C book. Nobody actually plays any of those things professionally."

A class discussion on the use of detail and interconnection of ideas might focus on the ways that Matthew Holicek and Karen Kramer organize and develop their topics. Each of these essays is a response to a different assignment — classification, extended definition, comparison and contrast — yet it is clear that the subject matter itself shaped the form and organization rather than the other way around. Students do not always understand this distinction and think that the real purpose in an assignment is to follow a model, something which unfortunately becomes tedious for both writer and reader. It is important to remind students that these various rhetorical devices are not an end in themselves but rather strategies that enhance focus and clarity.

## Further Suggestions for Reading, Writing, and Discussion

Margot Harrison's "Creative Transfiguration from the Death of a Moth" (page 201) is another excellent example of a comparison and contrast essay. Harrison makes an interesting point about the two essays she compares, stating that the essays had to prove to her that they deserved comparison. That is a point you might want to raise in class.

Donald Murray in *Write to Learn* (New York: Holt, Rinehart and Winston, 1984) suggests that one way to gather ideas for writing is to draw up an "authority list," a list of topics or subjects about which students are unquestionable authorities. Encourage students to have some fun with their list, perhaps by suggesting some topics: causing guilt, overeating, curing hiccups, making someone angry, forgetting things, postponing work.

Students might enjoy sharing some of these topics first in their writing response groups, thus allowing them to expand on the information. Then they might be assigned a rhetorical category — classification, extended definition, comparison and contrast — and asked to select the form that seems most appropriate to try their hand at detailing their expertise. Usually if someone is good at causing guilt, another student is equally competent at feeling guilty, and some rather comic cures can be arranged.

## Instructor's Comments: *Joan Griffin, University of Nebraska at Lincoln*

I don't much "cotton" to giving or offering advice to my colleagues! If pressed, I would say one thing we can do to encourage our students to write well is to try to build their confidence in themselves as users of language. I do think that those of us who try to "teach" writing must work hard to establish a nonthreatening writer's environment in our classrooms. And I say that because I am a firm believer in the doctrine that says that writing is a very public act. My students find out early in the semester that I am only *one* of their readers. When the chemistry is right I find that peer reaction/encouragement can be one of the most significant causes of effective writing.

I usually use small groups in my writing classes, sometimes as often as every third class meeting. Small group tasks range from brainstorming sessions for the next paper, reading/reacting to each other's drafts and final versions, to group writing assignments and other kinds of writing exercises. I have found that small groups work best when provided with a set of clearly defined instructions.

In line with my emphasis on audience awareness and writing as a public act, I regularly reproduce parts of or entire student papers for the whole class to read. I think that it is important for writers to see their work in print and to see their audience in the act of "decoding." Often, I will ask the small groups to decide which papers should be reproduced and why (the "why" directs our full class discussions).

**RICHARD SELZER**, "Letter to a Young Surgeon," page 300

**Teaching Strategies**

The particular use of metaphors that we emphasize in this unit — to distinguish between things that most people could not otherwise tell apart — is only part of what Selzer does with metaphors in his essay. He distinguishes among different kinds of surgeons most clearly in paragraphs 6–9, classifying them as "old lions," "tortoises," "swashbucklers," and "the rest of us." Selzer does not merely mention these metaphors and pass on; he builds on them. When he mentions old lions, he goes on to talk about blunted claws; when he refers to tortoises, he talks about a "field as bloodless as a cadaver" — a region devoid of liquid like the desert where tortoises live; when he speaks of swashbucklers, he refers to "slicker and boots," raingear worn on ships. These metaphors allow us to visualize what it is like to see a surgeon work and to enter into the feelings of surgeons as they work. They tell us in only the vaguest terms about specific techniques. Selzer is not concerned with precise technique; he believes that if a surgeon has the correct spirit and feelings about surgery, proper technique will follow easily.

Selzer can use a single metaphor to make several different, even somewhat contradictory, points. For example, he mentions Japanese artists in paragraph 7 to criticize the excessive cleanliness of some surgeons; then he says in a fanciful passage in paragraph 9 that all surgeons ought to be trained as thoroughly as Japanese artists are. He is ambivalent, then, about the precision required of surgeons. He does not want a mechanical mastery and so he prescribes practicing knot tying as a prelude to making love (paragraph 12). He also criticizes a doctor who removes his patient's navels to preserve the "pure line of his slice" as guilty of practicing aesthetics without love (paragraph 20).

Love is a recurring refrain in this essay (paragraphs 4, 12, 13, 22), and Selzer becomes quite physical in his descriptions. He advises surgeons, "You will not announce your love but will store it up in the bodies of your patients." But Selzer certainly regards the love he wants surgeons to have as a holy love, a religious love. He says, "you must operate with piety" (paragraph 13) and compares surgeons to gods, priests, and the biblical figure of Jonah (paragraphs 15, 17, 23, 26). He regards the godlike powers of the surgeon as the greatest danger; only by assuming the humility of a religious supplicant can a surgeon escape becoming arrogant.

It might be interesting to consider whether Selzer's advice to surgeons could be applied to his writing. He might criticize his writing for not being humble: he imposes his cleverness on his readers. He might regard some of his metaphors as rather sloppy, piling on top of one another. Some readers may wish Selzer would clean up and simplify his writing and not embellish every sentence with so many exotic metaphors. Selzer might, on the other hand, praise himself for writing with love, for bringing his whole soul into his prose, laying himself wide open for the reader.

**Connections to Other Essays**

For some thoughts on similarities among all the essays in this collection written by doctors, see the instructor's manual entry on "The Use of Force" by William Carlos Williams.

"The Right Stuff" by Tom Wolfe (page 353) attempts to define the ideal astronaut or test pilot; Selzer's essay could be considered an attempt to define the ideal surgeon. Selzer is seeking to describe the intangible "right stuff" that surgeons need. Selzer and Wolfe both discuss the issue of the egotism that accompanies being the best in a highly regarded profession. The pilots seem to revel in their glory, while Selzer says that humility is crucial to being a great surgeon. Students might discuss which view they prefer of how a great person should act. Are both views partly correct? Has Selzer minimized the bravado surgeons need to perform their daring feats? Would test pilots be better if they had the kind of humility Selzer describes?

"Shooting an Elephant" by George Orwell (page 82) deals with a man who finds himself in a position where he can think of himself as a god lording it over mere mortals. Orwell shows how such a position turns the mildest person into a tyrant. Selzer's essay attempts to counter the egotism that accompanies the great power and respect surgeons command. If we consider the surgeon as an imperialist invading the colony of the patient's body, many of Orwell's comments would apply to surgery (surgeons probably fear being laughed at by their patients, for example). Is it possible to define a kind of proper humility that would allow an imperial ruler to govern a colony without tyranny?

**DAVID G. LANDMANN,** "The House," page 309

Students and instructors alike will find a great deal to discuss in David Landmann's essay. Landmann has a complex purpose for writing his piece. This is not solely a study of an impoverished family; it is a tribute to the doughty nature of Isiah Lewis. The narrator's eye is the eye of the social photographer who directs the reader, through a careful selection of detail, to see the broader implication of poverty.

Unlike the objective, cinematic viewpoint we find in some documentaries on poverty, Landmann's point of view is committed, intense. Using the art of the camera, he gives us a close-up of Lewis's hand, of the rusting wired makeshift door. He directs our attention repeatedly to the crude paint-can privy, toward the brutalizing effect of neglect on "the oddly conceived family." With a sure hand, he captures portraits: "the ancient, one-eyed man; the odd-looking, stoop-shouldered young woman, holding an infant whose clothing was stained with its own excrement; the older children, whose hungry haunting eyes scanned the big cars on the street." These are pictures akin to the statements made by filmmakers and photographers in the early 1930s.

But Landmann's study makes us even more uncomfortable. This scene does not take place during the Depression and the setting is not some forgotten tobacco road. The cardboard shack is situated a few feet from a major intersection in the heart of an affluent society of the 1980s.

The essay might legitimately have become a sermon on the inhumanity of societal neglect. Instead, Landmann exhibits admirable restraint. He makes the shack the focal point of for his message. We view the fragile existence of the Isiah Lewis family through the "water-warped, refrigerator-carton walls" of the cardboard "house." We feel the distress of each of the seasons: winter is " 'the wustest time' . . . because you 'can't put no cookstove in no cardbo'd house.' " The shack becomes the symbol of poverty, not merely an aspect of it. It is important to draw students' attention to the control that Landmann exerts here, as it will provide them with an opportunity to uncover their own symbol-making power to express abstract ideas.

Another strength of the essay is that Landmann allows Lewis to tell his own story. The narrator has a nearly faultless ear for hearing voice and an equally competent hand for transposing speech into writing. We recognize that many of the points in the essay emerge directly from Lewis's comments, which gives Landmann's argument added substance. A class hour might be spent profitably examining how dialogue adds dramatic dimension to the portraits students wish to create. You might ask them to look at Celeste Barrus's essay "Todd" (page 47), in which the same principle is at work.

"The House" is also a study in contrast and contradiction. Although the invisibility of the poor is Landmann's theme, he does not always talk about it directly. Rather, the reader comes to see the idea through a series of observations made by the narrator and Lewis. At every turn the Lewis family ought to have been noticed. The house is at a major intersection, yet "its images were not allowed to register." The agencies that might have helped them — the church, the welfare and health boards — seem to have overlooked their existence. Even when the Lewises are forced to scavenge from the town dump or from the hopper behind the supermarket, eyes are averted. Students will be interested in how concretely the point is made without the use of the word "invisible." Note Lewis's explanation of how the family manages to scrounge its meager living: "Dat ol' watcherman at the dump, he be blin' or sumpin'. . . . It's jus' like I ain't there"; "If the white folks sees them babies, dey jus' don't say nuthin' nohow." Even the newspaper reporter who brings the story to the public fails to escape the indictment.

The introduction of the reporter at the end of the essay points out a problem in the narrative role. The narrator's connection to the story is not entirely clear. We assume that he is an observer who has taken the time to talk to Isiah Lewis. But we never discover, not even at the conclusion, that Landmann was the photographer who accompanied the reporter on the day that a flat tire brought them to the Lewises' shack. Certainly we recognize the art of the photographer in the details that are presented, but it would help the reader if the narrator had explained at the beginning his share in the experience. This information, partly in coming at the end, falls a bit flat. But this is a small quibble in an otherwise beautifully wrought study.

## Further Suggestions for Reading, Writing, and Discussion

Henry David Thoreau, in *Walden,* describes the purchase of a shanty from a laborer on the Fitchburg railroad in Massachusetts. Nineteenth-century writer Thoreau bought the shanty to erect in the woods. He portrays it in this fashion:

> By the middle of April, for I made no haste in my work, but rather made the most of it, my house was framed and ready for the raising. I had already bought the shanty of James Collins, an Irishman who worked on the Fitchburg Railroad, for boards. James Collins' shanty was considered an uncommonly fine one. When I called to see it he was not at home. I walked about the outside, at first unobserved from within, the window was so deep and high. It was of small dimensions, with a peaked cottage roof, and not much else to be seen, the dirt being raised five feet all around as if it were a compost heap. The roof was the soundest part, though a good deal warped and made brittle by the sun. Doorsill there was none, but a perennial passage for the hens under the door-board. Mrs. C. came to the door and asked me to view it from the inside. The hens were driven in by my approach. It was dark, and had a dirt floor for the most part, dank, clammy,

and aguish, only here a board and there a board which would not bear removal. She lighted a lamp to show me the inside of the roof and the walls, and also that the board floor extended under the bed, warning me not to step into the cellar, a sort of dust hole two feet deep. In her own words, they were "good boards overhead, good boards all around, and a good window," — of two whole squares originally, only the cat had passed out that way lately. There was a stove, a bed, and a place to sit, an infant in the house where it was born, a silk parasol, gilt-framed looking-glass, and a patent new coffee-mill nailed to an oak sapling, all told. The bargain was soon concluded, for James had in the meanwhile returned. I to pay four dollars and twenty-five cents to-night, he to vacate at five to-morrow morning, selling to nobody else meanwhile: I to take possession at six. It were well, he said, to be there early, and anticipate certain indistinct but wholly unjust claims on the score of ground rent and fuel. This he assured me was the only encumbrance. At six I passed him and his family on the road. One large bundle held their all, — bed, coffee-mill, looking-glass, hens, — all but the cat; she took to the woods and became a wild cat, and, as I learned afterward, trod in a trap set for woodchucks, and so became a dead cat at last.

I took down this dwelling the same morning, drawing the nails, and removed it to the pond-side by small cart-loads, spreading the boards on the grass there to bleach and warp back again in the sun. One early thrush gave me a note or two as I drove along the woodland path. I was informed treacherously by a young Patrick that neighbor Seeley, an Irishman, in the intervals of the carting, transferred the still tolerable, straight, and drivable nails, staples, and spikes to his pocket, and then stood when I came back to pass the time of day, and look freshly up, unconcerned, with spring thoughts, at the devastation: there being a dearth of work, as he said. He was there to represent spectatordom, and help make this seemingly insignificant event one with the removal of the gods of Troy.

I dug my cellar in the side of a hill sloping to the south, where a woodchuck had formerly dug his burrow, down through sumach and black-berry roots, and the lowest stain of vegetation, six feet square by seven deep, to a fine sand where potatoes would not freeze in any winter. The sides were left shelving, and not stoned; but the sun having never shone on them, the sand still keeps its place. It was but two hours' work. I took particular pleasure in this breaking of ground, for in almost all latitudes men dig into the earth for an equable temperature. Under the most splendid house in the city is still to be found the cellar where they store their roots as of old, and long after the superstructure has disappeared posterity remark its dent in the earth. The house is still but a sort of porch at the entrance of a burrow.

At length, in the beginning of May, with the help of some of my acquaintances, rather to improve so good an occasion for neighborliness than from any necessity, I set up the frame of my house. No man was ever more honored in the character of his raisers than I. They are destined, I trust, to assist at the raising of loftier structures one day. I began to occupy my house on the 4th of July, as soon as it was boarded and roofed, for the boards were carefully feather-edged and lapped, so that it was perfectly impervious to rain, but before boarding I laid the foundation of a chimney at one end, bringing two cartloads of stones up the hill from the pond in my arms. I built the chimney after my hoeing in the fall, before a fire became necessary for warmth, doing my cooking in the meanwhile out of doors on the ground, early in the morning: which mode I still think is in some respects more convenient and agreeable than the usual one. When it stormed before my bread was baked, I fixed a few boards over the fire, and sat under them to watch my loaf, and passed some pleasant hours in that way. In those days, when my hands were much employed, I read but little, but the least scraps of paper which lay on the ground, my holder, or tablecloth, afforded me as much entertainment, in fact answered the same purpose as the *Iliad.*

An interesting class discussion would center on the role of the two shacks — those of Lewis and of Thoreau — in the lives of these two men. In Lewis's case, the shack was a symbol of the poverty forced on his family when society abandoned them. In Thoreau's case, it was a conscious renunciation.

## Instructor's Comments: *Richard Rulkerson, East Texas State University*

David's essay is distinguished by many features: a sure eye for telling detail; an excellent use of dialogue; a maturity of insight; and a sincere, mature personal voice. All of these elements are focused on moving a reader to share the writer's experience and reaction to it.

**FRANCIS DANA BARKER GAGE,** "Sojourner Truth: And A'n't I a Woman?" page 315

### Teaching Strategies

Francis Gage wishes to prove that women can be as strong as men. She could have presented scientific evidence of women's muscular power, but in an essay the strength that can be most directly demonstrated is the strength of words. So Gage creates a scene in which we can ourselves hear a "voice . . . like rolling thunder." When Sojourner Truth stands up in the crowd, there is a "profound hush" as every other voice falls silent. We too feel awe in the presence of a towering heroic figure. Sojourner modestly pretends to have but a "little half-measure full" of intelligence, but she is witty enough to twist Eve's original sin into evidence that one woman is "strong enough to turn de world upside down all alone." Sojourner's dialect and race make it clear that her intelligence and verbal skills are not the result of the educational system but rather represent the raw material being wasted by that system when it excludes women and blacks.

This essay is an example of very effective use of quotations; Gage sets up Sojourner's speech very skillfully to increase its dramatic impact. She describes two kinds of arguments that Sojourner answers: arguments by leaders of the women's movement that Sojourner should not be allowed to speak and arguments by men against women's rights. The leaders of the women's movement are afraid that letting a black woman speak about women's rights will cloud the issue, bringing abolition into the discussion. Gage suggests that these white women are not as eager for racial as for sexual equality. The writer herself believes that the two issues cannot be separated — equality must come to all people. Gage parallels the fears of the other women and the men in the audience, so that the essay speaks not only to men but to women who want to limit liberation (women who would say, "Liberation will mean all women will think and speak and look as we do"). The problem of whether liberation can come to one group without coming to all remains today: women's rights groups and civil rights groups remain separate and sometimes quarrel.

Sojourner's first words directly respond to the women's fears; she points out that blacks and women have a common enemy — white men. Sojourner's stately demeanor and eloquence further show that the women need not have worried — she is a better advocate of women's issues than the leaders themselves. Even before Sojourner speaks, Gage counters the fears of the leaders by describing

Sojourner as an impressive figure, a "Lybian Statue," an "Amazon." These terms might spark some controversy in class, because they have a racist and sexist tinge today. No modern white writer would describe a tall black woman as a Lybian Amazon. It is hard to tell what connotations those words had in the nineteenth century. They do suggest that Gage regards Sojourner as something of an exotic, "foreign" person, not simply as an American, but Gage may merely be trying to make Sojourner seem extraordinary, superhuman.

Sojourner's speech directly answers the arguments against women's rights given by men earlier in the essay. By considering how carefully Gage sets up the beginning so that Sojourner answers precisely those points that the men raise, students will see that this is a well-structured argumentative essay, not merely a dramatic scene. This essay could be rewritten without the characters as a general consideration of women's rights, starting with a series of arguments against equality that are then countered. Students could discuss what is added by actually dramatizing the debate. Many of Sojourner's rhetorical strategies would be difficult to include in a straightforward essay (such as acting modest about her intelligence while brilliantly cutting up the men's arguments).

One of the basic strategies of persuasion is to convince readers that the writer is a trustworthy person. Note how Gage creates two trustworthy "writers" — Sojourner and herself. Sojourner's personal traits, as revealed in her speech — intelligence, physical and moral strength, courage, wit, charisma — serve as powerful arguments in themselves for women's and blacks' equality. Gage can bring those qualities into her essay without presenting herself as possessing them, without seeming egotistical. She presents herself modestly, as not much of a speaker and not too sure of herself. Her best qualities seem to be her even temper and her willingness to listen to all sides. She is a figure that we as readers can identify with, a moderator who has moderate moral courage and moderate intelligence. Gage shows us that by creating a character to speak the most powerful arguments in an essay, we can in essence have two narrators in one paper, one passionate and impressive, the other reasonable, calm, and modest.

At the end, Gage places herself in a group with her readers when she says that Sojourner "had taken us up in her strong arms and carried us safely over the slough of difficulty turning the whole tide in our favor." Gage is being quite modest — it is her own writing that has carried her readers along; moreover, Gage has set up the essay so that we first feel the tide going against "us" and then dramatically shifting when Sojourner speaks. Gage also deserves credit for re-creating Sojourner's voice — most persons who listened to Sojourner would never have been able to create in writing such a compelling speaker.

## Connections to Other Essays

"A Letter of the Times" by Alice Walker (page 266) also discusses the interrelationship between feminism and racism and also uses characters to represent the author's point.

For notes about essays that discuss the experiences of ethnic minorities, see the instructor's manual entry on Maxine Hong Kingston's "The Woman Warrior."

**PATRICK KINDER LEWIS,** "Five Minutes North of Redding," page 320

## Teaching Strategies

Patrick Kinder Lewis's essay was a response to an assignment to take an experience in life and "shape it carefully into a polished essay." About the assignment, Lewis writes, "Essays aren't supposed to be very long. So I wanted to simply re-create the painting of that moment which I have carried around mentally for the last four years. But there was the problem of making those characters looking out the door of that boxcar into men who lived and breathed." One of his concerns, therefore, was condensing the experience yet at the same time rendering both the men and the journey in some manner that would "create the snapshot which I took of that epiphanic moment."

The essay divides itself into three stages. The first deals with getting on and getting settled on the train; the second, with the meeting with Alex; and the third, with the trip itself and the camaraderie that developed among Lewis, Alex, and the Beaners. But the heart of the essay is the "epiphanic" moment, the moment when the train crosses the trestle over the Sacramento River. It is this "snapshot" that Lewis wanted to explore by writing about it, recognizing even at the moment how he would be haunted by this scene: "Like a stolen glimpse of childbirth, I shared in that peaceful feeling of something both beginning and ending at once. And like a mother smiling at her child born at last, I found myself smiling with a similar relief. It was joy without euphoria. I hunted again for the insights of the moment before but found them fading with the darkness of the mountains ahead. What race had I run to earn such rest? What was born in that moment?"

The first part of the essay focuses primarily on the writer, his insights and feelings, as well as setting the stage for the moment to come. The details of the narration are spare but telling. Lewis does not merely recount what he sees. Continually throughout the essay, he is intent on understanding the larger meaning: for example, when he describes the men playing in the plum trees, "I watched intently, as if it were some elaborate social experiment, until the sound of boots on gravel brought me back around." The second part introduces his traveling companions and gives readers a sense of the hazards that he has undertaken. Again, readers are taken into Lewis's confidence as he explains his decision to join Alex, whose description reflects Lewis's ability to undergo experience at the same time he moves it to a higher understanding: "And he just looked tough. . . . Very tough but somehow gentle. He seemed all in all an atavism, a confusing mixture of General Custer with a sixties flower child." Attention should be brought to this aspect of the narrative because the writer is concerned not only with the excitement of what he is doing but also with how it fits into a larger scheme. This larger vision is what moves the essay into an abstraction about human experience. A dual point of view is in constant operation: through Lewis's telling of events we witness what is happening to Lewis and the others; through the reflections of the mind's eye the events are enlarged and given meaning.

This aspect of the narrative is most clearly defined in the last section of the essay, when the continuum of the journey is stopped and the moment on the trestle reveals both the end and the beginning of the train. Lewis has an eye that frames scenes; indeed, he writes in scenes. The journey gives way to a stage setting in which the trestle and the train become actors. The descriptions are of a high order, carefully crafted so that readers will understand that this is not just another beautiful view on an unusual journey. Lewis does not pretend to understand the grace that operates; rather he lets his readers share his joy and his confusion. It was, he says elsewhere, "the fulfillment of a youthful dream and the beginning of a more mature vision."

For an example of the student editing process, see the discussion of Lewis's essay in Chapter 2, "Peer Editing."

## Further Suggestions for Reading, Writing, and Discussion

An essay by Edward Hoagland, "The Midnight Freight to Portland," which appears in various essay collections, views the railroads from another perspective.

Riding as a guest of the railroad, Hoagland focuses on railroad personnel and problems, offering developed sketches of the towns the trains pass, the life that people live on the railroad. An interesting discussion should grow out of the different purposes for each essay — Hoagland wants a share in the mythology and romance of railroading even though he does not want "to go as a hobo," whereas Lewis never uses the term "hobo" nor explains exactly why he has taken his railroad journey.

*Journey* is another word for "quest." What Lewis seeks is never explained. The reader infers that a search for the self takes place. At some point, students have undoubtedly undertaken, perhaps on a more limited basis, such a search or journey. Thoreau undertook his quest in Concord. An interesting assignment that might grow out of this essay is to ask students to recount some time in their lives when they went away by themselves. To remove the writing from the realm of travelogue or "How I Enjoyed My Summer Vacation," ask students to notice the absence of specific reasons in the Lewis essay, the way in which the opening paragraph does not "introduce" the quest in the usual way but rather places the reader in the middle of the experience and lets the reader draw whatever inferences are necessary. This assignment will be useful for helping students shape and focus narrative. What they discover in terms of growth and changing values will be as important as the description of the experience itself.

## Instructor's Comments: *Sharon Ewert, Wheaton College*

Most of the really good writers that I have had have also been good readers. My advice would be to read widely, read carefully, and be sensitive not only to the content of what you read but also to the sound, to the way an author puts words together. Then as you write, aim above everything else for a style that is clear, direct, and uniquely your own. Forget the "academic sound" that you hear so often in textbooks and research papers, and work instead for a style that is vivid and alive, a style where you not only actively choose the subject and the organization but also carefully shape the paragraphing, the sentence patterns, and the cadence of words.

Too often we as teachers of writing tend to emphasize the small, technical matters or to focus on what is wrong in a paper. Hearing only the bad — or, worse yet, getting a paper back with only a grade and few if any marks on it — causes students to get discouraged easily and to begin to believe that they simply cannot write. I find that most of my job is being a coach, helping them to correct what is weak, but first of all helping them to see their strengths. Once I have built up their confidence in themselves, I try to give them a vision of what good writing can be and then try to help them work toward that ideal.

## ANNIE DILLARD, "Death of a Moth," page 330

### Teaching Strategies

Dillard's essay revolves entirely around the intensely described symbol at its center — a burning moth. The first section of the essay is amusing, pleasant, full of everyday thoughts. The middle rises in intensity very rapidly, reaching a peak of emotion that might even make some readers feel Dillard is losing her mind as she stares at the burning moth. The last section returns to the pleasant, mild prose of the beginning. The three-part structure takes us through the experience of being struck by the power of a symbol; wandering through daily life, we are surprised for a short time by overpowering emotions and then dropped back into our normal state. Even if students do not recognize the "meanings" that Dillard packs into the description of the moth, they should recognize that Dillard creates an incredibly intense image that is so "heavy" that it demands interpretation and drives us to reread the essay. We have to think hard to figure out what this burning moth might mean to Dillard. That is the nature of symbols, as we experience them in real life — something stands out as affecting us very powerfully, out of proportion to its seeming importance in our lives, and we have to think hard to figure out why it affects us so strongly.

Since Dillard has chosen to surround her description of the burning moth with comments on her life, we can assume that she sees some connection between the moth and her life. Her descriptions repeatedly parallel her life and the burning moth, most strikingly when she says that she herself was "kindled" by the light of the burning moth. She is on fire herself, and we know the fire that is burning her when she compares herself to Rimbaud, who "burnt out his brain in a thousand poems." The moth's head burns intensely; so does an inspired poet, on fire with ideas and images he or she has to write. Further enriching the comparison of moth and poet are all the religious references, suggesting that devotion to poetry is like devotion to God. Poets retreat from the world to pursue inspiration, just as saints and virgins do.

Once the paralleling of poet/monk/moth is clear, the rest of this essay becomes eminently interpretable. Almost every detail of Dillard's seemingly bland description of her life suggests deeper meaning. The spider who eats bugs and throws their wrinkled carcasses on the floor is like a writer tossing his or her rejected drafts on the ground. Dillard's comment at the end that she thinks it "pretty funny" that she sleeps alone points to the ambivalence she feels about her choice to be an acolyte of the religion of writing. The phrase "pretty funny" also makes us think about the various kinds of humor in this essay. Dillard uses a dry wit in describing her own life, lightly laughing at herself. Some readers may also find humor in the intense description of the moth because it is so excessive and grotesque. We could laugh at the burning moth as we laugh at horror movies when a terrifying sound turns out to be a cat jumping out of a closet. Dillard's moth is both horrifying and nonthreatening, and so possibly funny.

Students might regard this essay as a kind of puzzle, but Dillard does not think of her writing that way. She says, "Young writers must be relieved endlessly of the notion that the critic's role is to 'find the hidden meaning,' and the writer's is to hide them, like Easter eggs." Dillard would presumably argue that she is less interested in the critical act of finding hidden meanings in her writing than in the effect of the symbolic images she creates. The point is not to come away with the right answer, but to feel a bit burned as a reader by the intensity of Dillard's prose. She wants us to remember that burning moth much more than any intellectual interpretation of it. However, the intellectual "content" of the symbol is essential to its power. The moth is so vivid because it is so powerfully transformed by Dillard's words — into a "gold tube," a monk, a "flame-faced virgin." Dillard's comments on symbols and how they work (quoted in the headnote) might spark discussion of this essay. She says that art probes a region where "blurred and powerful symbols are the only speech." Does the symbol in this essay speak in ways no other words could? Dillard also says that symbols are "exploratory craft" in which we "leave the planet." Does this essay take us off this planet? If so, where does it take us?

Students may discover that developing their own symbols is very difficult. Not any object or image can be described in grand terms and thereby become "meaningful." Some students may find they are very uncomfortable using symbols; others may think it is a fascinating and natural way to write. It might be useful to point out that many great writers avoid symbols. Dillard herself divides writing into two basic styles, "fine" and "plain." Fine writing is full of symbols, using elaborate description and exotic phrases to add layers of meaning to ordinary objects. Dillard says fine writing "lays no claims to precision. It is an energy. It sacrifices perfect control to ambition to mean." In contrast, "the short sentences of plain prose have a good deal of blank space around them." Plain prose "flaunts its simplicity . . . [and] has one supreme function, which is not to call attention to itself, but to refer to the world." Students might try to identify their own styles as tending toward "fine" or "plain" writing.

## Connections to Other Essays

Dillard's essay invites comparison with Virginia Woolf's "The Death of the Moth" (page 397). Dillard may have consciously sought to echo Woolf's title. By examining the radically different ways the two authors deal with the same small event, students can become aware of how a writer transforms his or her material. Margot Harrison's essay "Creative Transfiguration from the Death of a Moth" (page 201) provides a superb analysis of the Dillard and Woolf essays. These three essays could be used to structure a sequence of assignments: (1) students build their own symbolic essays, modeling their works on Dillard's and Patrick Kinder Lewis's; (2) students write short analyses of each other's symbols and discuss which ones seem to work and which seem forced or artificial; (3) students write complete literary critical essays about a piece that contains a symbol (perhaps about their own symbolic works or about professional works such as James Joyce's "Araby" [page 507] or Robert Frost's "Design" [page 207]).

"Shooting an Elephant" by George Orwell (page 82) might be considered a "symbolic" essay like Dillard's. Students can discuss whether the elephant and Orwell's act of shooting it are "symbols" or simply "examples" of some general theme.

## THOMAS LEYBA, "The Marfa Lights," page 335

## Teaching Strategies

Leyba's fascinating research into the mysterious lights of Marfa began prior to the semester in which he wrote the essay. Leyba's decision to educate his readers about this curious phenomenon is clearly tied both to his passion for West Texas and to the opportunity the subject provided him to become directly involved: "To learn of the Bermuda Triangle, I could simply conduct research in a library and learn about this long-distance phenomenon. If I had to travel abroad to learn of it, I would remain ignorant. Let's just say that, with my essay, I spare you an expensive trip and bring the Marfa Lights to you, reader."

Diane Kocour's description of the process by which she arrived at her topic emphasizes her decision to try to distance her experience from the inquiry. Leyba makes no such claim; rather, he wants his readers "to feel what I felt." Part of the success of the essay derives from his emphasis on the emotional nature of the story: "The idea of what I wanted to say began to develop the first night I saw the Lights. I knew I wanted an authentic essay — one brought to life by people with a history in Marfa. I wanted to feel what Marfans felt when they spoke of the Lights."

Accordingly, the essay emphasizes the testimony of the various people who have seen the lights, beginning with an extended quotation from a story in *Texas Monthly*, the narrative of which sets the tone for the rest of the essay. Students should note the effective manner with which Leyba introduces his subject. By using a columnist from a presumably widely read publication, Leyba lends both interest and credibility to the difficult job that lies ahead. Leyba also cites extensively local folklorists such as Mr. Vasquez, who has gathered a vast storehouse of anecdotes and history over the years.

The essay contains many stories within stories, and it may prove a bit confusing to readers as Leyba shifts back and forth between historical accounts, eyewitness sightings, and scientific explanations. In many ways the essay violates the rules of organization. Occasionally Leyba interrupts the narrative to suggest a different direction, as in paragraph 10 when he urges us to "leave him [Fritz Kahl] and his reported adventure in the high dark for a moment and turn to the supernatural." Leyba promises a road map — a discussion of the two sets of legends peculiar to the older and younger generations of viewers — as well as some scientific explanation. Thus he launches into a fairly full discussion of the kinds of myths that have surrounded the Lights, helping readers considerably in paragraph 19 when he reintroduces Fritz Kahl briefly: "Once again, returning to aviator Fritz Kahl's account." But the organization of the information does not always fall easily into any category and readers become intensely dependent on Leyba for reminders and clarifications that are not always forthcoming. We do not always know who the experts are and we sometimes forget if we have met them earlier. A discussion of the essay might provide an opportunity to talk about organization as well as that crucial process of identifying sources in the body of the essay. Where the presentation is of necessity discursive, the writer does encounter problems of order, and students might appreciate an opportunity to analyze someone else's struggles.

Given the diversity and number of accounts, ask students if they are able to draw some conclusion about the origin of the Lights. Ask them in particular to look at the ending of the essay and judge whether the ending satisfies us. Has the author offered a last word on the subject? Should he?

## Further Suggestions for Reading, Writing, and Discussion

In the instructor's manual entry on Bonnie Harris's "The Healing Power of Music," the use of a descriptive outline is explained. It might be interesting for students to attempt such an outline to understand the organizational problems of Leyba's essay. Ask students if they see any other means of ordering or developing ideas that might provide readers with the clues necessary to follow his argument.

Students might consider the rich resource that lies at their fingertips by undertaking research in local history. Neighbors, often overlooked as experts, may provide fascinating background and detail. In many communities, libraries have begun accumulating information from local people in the form of oral histories. Such histories may be a good place to begin a study.

## Instructor's Comments: *Martha Connolly, University of Texas, El Paso*

To generate quality student essays, we should keep doing what we've done in the past that worked. Also, use many small group workshops for revising purposes.

## TOM WOLFE, "The Right Stuff," page 353

### Teaching Strategies

Tom Wolfe has made a whole book out of a series of stories that are all variations on a simple theme: each one is an example of how men with "the right stuff" act. Each story seems almost sufficient in itself to define "the right stuff," but the sum total of all the stories makes us understand that the right stuff is something that exceeds any given story, any given act: to have the right stuff is to participate in a "seemingly infinite series of tests," as if one were "climbing one of those ancient Babylonian pyramids made up of a dizzy progression of steps and ledges, a ziggurat, a pyramid." Wolfe's stories form a ziggurat for readers to ascend; he makes us dizzy as each tale carries us farther up the pyramid, closer to the "very Brotherhood of the Right Stuff," and we begin to feel how lame and worthless are the words that supposedly define or evaluate this quality. We know what bravery is, but then we are placed on a heaving carrier watching an airplane "*falling* . . . headed not for a stripe on the deck but for *me* — and with a horrible *smash!*" We begin to wonder whether the right stuff is insanity, stupidity, crass egotism, or saintliness. If students try to state what Wolfe's attitude is toward these pilots, they will see how he continually shifts his tone. He admires them; he thinks they are immature fools; he worries about being "left behind"; he is happy to take risks with words and not with his skin. As we read, we know more and more what this "stuff" is, and we see more and more that is indefinable, mysterious.

Much of the dizzying effect of Wolfe's prose comes from his sentences, as we can see most clearly in paragraph 11, where we roll and fall and splash and feel ourselves both inside a plane landing on a carrier and on the deck with the plane coming right at us. Wolfe's sentences do not simply state an idea, they move like roller coasters — going into italics, using exclamation points, switching point of view, shifting level of diction, disappearing into ellipses.

Wolfe makes us feel that his stories are taking us "higher" in several senses. At the end he uses the literal height of the pilots above the earth metaphorically, to suggest they have left common humanity behind. To be above others is to be superior. He has provided us with a long list of ways that persons are "left behind," and the few who survive to the end of this essay stand on quite a heap of bodies. Finally, Wolfe ascends all the way into the heavens, to that highest of all persons, God — and the pilots even put God in second place, as "co-pilot." Students might discuss all the ways that physical height serves metaphorically in our society (church spires, upward mobility, and so on).

Wolfe uses certain key phrases repeatedly — "the right stuff," "left behind." This essay can be analyzed as a musical work; these phrases would be refrains or, to use a term of Wolfe's own, "motifs" (paragraph 9). Students might discuss how important rhythms and sound effects are in this essay. Wolfe wants us to get carried away with his sentences and with the flow of the whole piece. The rhythms and repetitions set up very strong expectations of what will come next, and yet Wolfe keeps varying the way he presents his stories to hold our interest and surprise us. He alternates stories of courage and stories of foolishness, leaving us in suspense about how to finally think of the pilots; note how late in the essay he mentions deaths by automobiles (paragraph 27). He unifies the chapter by starting and ending with talk of death (and what is beyond life). These structural and musical effects make reading the essay a physical experience as well as a mental one.

Wolfe says that the pilots speak of the right stuff only in code or by example. Some readers might feel that Wolfe violates the spirit of the pilots by discussing the right stuff openly. However, this essay could be seen as consisting of only examples and coded statements. The phrase "the right stuff" is little more than a code, and when Wolfe speaks just about the "stuff" a man has, we can see how the word serves only to point to something, but not to define it. The stories are clearly examples and are much more important in this essay than Wolfe's occasional direct discussion of what the right stuff is. A class might discuss the odd moment in paragraph 24 when Wolfe lists the words that pilots never uttered — "*death, danger, bravery, fear.*" Is he really "uttering" them, or is he himself making us think how inadequate they are to describe the right stuff?

## Connections to Other Essays

In paragraph 14, Wolfe says that "there was something ancient, primordial, irresistible about the challenge of this stuff, no matter what a sophisticated and rational age one might think he lived in." In "On Boxing" (page 187), Joyce Carol Oates also discusses the contrast between the primordial and the rational and also focuses on masculinity and facing death as primordial qualities. She makes much of the fact that boxing does not involve words, just as Wolfe makes much of the pilots' never speaking of the right stuff. Students might discuss the fascination so many writers have with inarticulate persons who live dangerous, violent lives. Does language elevate us above violence, mask our violence, or simply provide us new forms of violence?

"On Killing the Man" by John Clyde Thatcher (page 515) might be taken as answering Tom Wolfe and Joyce Carol Oates. Thatcher does not see anything particularly mystical about killing; he suggests that the violence associated with manhood is not only unnecessary but possibly immoral.


**BRAD MANNING,** "Arm-Wrestling with My Father," page 369

## Teaching Strategies

Manning's essay is interesting not only for its description of a family ritual but for the imagery that underlies the narration. Manning explains in his question- naire how he came to see the experience in his mind's eye as a variation on the myth of Aeneas: "I got stuck on a dominant image, that of carrying my father on my back, as if this were to be a universal symbol of the changeover of strength and command from father to son. I thought it worked nicely with the deer metaphor, though it was not expressed clearly. But I took it too far, I think, when I universal- ized the action by invoking the image of Aeneas bearing his father Anchises on his back." He explains further that he decided to drop the comparison, except as it appears in the imagined scene of his father collapsing: "And in that second vision, I see me rushing to him, lifting him onto my shoulders, and running." The theme of the deer is also transmogrified into the analogy of the fish, structuring the recognition that when we win, we also lose.

On one level, then, the essay is about a family ritual, but on another it is really about the "changeover" that Manning notes. The ritual is characterized by its physicality. Readers have no doubt that the father overwhelms the son with his own ambitions. While this is a frequent theme of student literature, students often find it difficult to convey dramatically the force of the relationship and resort to summarizing events and feelings. Manning is adroit at illustrating his father's dominance in numerous ways: his strong hugs, his angry looks, the absence of words, his disappointment at lacrosse games. The father's arms become the domi- nant image in the essay from the moment the wrestling begins to the moment the father hugs his son goodbye at the airport. But the image of the arm is more than just a developed detail, it is also the focusing metaphor for the essay, providing Manning with a means to signal the changeover. The turning point occurs when Manning notices he is "becoming less my father and more myself." The insight is reflected in a comparison of their two arms: his father's "hairy and white with some pink moles scattered about," his own "lanky and featureless." The shift in power is signaled by the analogy of the fish: "Arm-wrestling my father was now like this, like hooking 'Big Joe,' the old fish that Lake Ouachita holds but you can never catch, and when you finally think you got him, you want to let him go, cut the line, keep the legend alive."

It is that kind of insight that laces the essay with far more meaning than the events themselves. This is important to point out to students. Our feelings about an experience, not the experience itself, keep the experience forward in our minds. Often when students write about such events, they seem to get lost in explaining what happened rather than what they have come to understand from it. Manning examines the other side of his father's strength — the shelter from life that the arms have offered — and the loss he now feels. The feeling is dramatized again in the scene at the airport when he finally comes to recognize how much his father loves him.

## Further Suggestions for Reading, Writing, and Discussion

Numerous essays in the various editions of *Student Writers at Work* deal with relationships between children and fathers:  in the first edition, Joanne Menter, "Home Is Where the Heart Is"; in the second edition, Amber Kennish, "Three Rounds with Dad"; in this third edition, Barbara Seidel, "A Tribute to My Father."

Some essays in this edition also deal with rituals: John Clyde Thatcher, "On Killing the Man"; Terry L. Burns, "The Blanket Party"; Ann Louise Field, "The Sound of Angels."

Each of the essays in some manner touches on the inevitable responsibility we must all assume when the rituals of childhood fail us. A good writing assignment might grow out of dramatizing how each student came to recognize when that moment came.

## Instructor's Comments: *Jack Kimball, Harvard University*

Good writing makes a point. Good writing argues.

Revise, revise. Revision is key in mastering writing.

Keep a journal. You should record your thoughts and observations regularly. As you read, for example, a good way to sift through new information is to take notes on your reactions, questions, and frustrations. You will find your journal is a primary source to generate ideas for writing.

## SCOTT RUSSELL SANDERS, "The Inheritance of Tools," page 379

### Teaching Strategies

Scott Sanders's essay opens with the death of his father; this death creates a problem that the rest of the essay attempts to solve. The death has interrupted the continuity of generations, the passing of life, love, culture from parent to child that forms the stable base for the narrator's own life. Tools serve to reestablish the continuity that has been interrupted. By writing, the narrator is nailing together the cultural planks on which he stands, covering over the hole created by the absence of his father.

Many of us, trying to keep alive a relationship with someone who died, would turn to memories of conversations and kisses. Sanders turns to memories of tools. We might speculate on why he makes this choice: perhaps because his father did not speak of his emotions, or perhaps because he knows that writing directly about love and intimacy is very difficult. If Sanders tried to explain how he loved his father and how his father loved him, especially while he is overwhelmed by the intense emotions he feels immediately after hearing of his father's death, the essay might bog down in generalities, or he might simply cry or scream.

By focusing on the specifics of tools, Sanders can find a channel for his emotions, a way to let them out in controlled ways so that they become engraved in his words almost indirectly, but more powerfully than they would be represented by talk of love and loss. Note that most of Sanders's comments on people and relationships are placed as small parts of sentences about tools, often prepositional phrases. For example, in paragraph 3, the central traits of his grandfather and father are presented almost as afterthoughts in a description of wood: "the grain in hickory is crooked and knotty, and therefore tough, hard to split, like the grain in the two men who owned this hammer before me." Or his grandfather's marriage comes as an introductory prepositional phrase (in paragraph 4): "After proposing marriage to a neighbor girl, my grandfather used this hammer to build a house."

Probably the best example of placing emotions off on the side is the opening sentence, where Sanders uses the news of his father's death to introduce the banging of his thumb: "At just about the hour when my father died, . . . I banged my thumb with a hammer." Banging his thumb seems a consciously symbolic act, an expression of anger at his father's death, though the narrator denies that, saying that the banging only coincidentally accompanied news of his father's death. In the paragraph, though, the scar that results becomes a symbol of death — a moon rising and eventually sinking across his thumbnail. Later in the essay, Sanders continues paralleling his reactions to his bruised thumb and to his father's death: in paragraph 27, he mentions pacing around the house "on fire" after hearing of his father's death and then switches to his anger at his bruised thumb, wishing he could "bury the shameful thing." He wants to bury his painful emotions (perhaps even ashamed of them, as males sometimes are), but mostly he wishes he could have the perfect order of a skillful world, where accidents and uncontrollable events such as deaths would not occur.

By making precise descriptions of tools the main clauses of his sentences and using general comments on people and even on all of civilization in subordinate parts, Sanders creates the effect of looking through small details to very general ideas — in other words, he makes his details symbolic. Instead of telling us directly about the importance of morality, tradition, and honesty in human relations, Sanders can say, "There is an unspoken morality in seeking the level and the plumb. A house will stand, a table will bear weight . . . only if the joints are square and the members upright" (paragraph 16). He seems to be speaking about physical forces and pieces of wood, but this sentence also says that the various "houses" we construct out of people (such as families or the House of Representatives) will "stand" and not fall apart only if "the members" — the individuals making them up — are "upright" and on the "level." He may even be saying that the best kind of morality is unspoken, made not of words but of the stands people take. When he says that the internal joints that no one "except a wrecking crew" will ever see must still be "square," he implies that the inner joints in people, their basic constitution, physical and mental, must be square, though these inner joints will be revealed only after their death to the "wrecking crew" of relatives and friends and perhaps God.

Sanders has a larger purpose in writing this essay than merely dealing with his own emotions. He wants to establish the continuity between the present society and all the previous generations back to the Stone Age. As Sanders says about this essay (quoted in the headnote), "I tell of my father's death because it focused for me lessons about the virtue and fragility of human skill." Sanders wants to speak about the continuity of human skills — we are using the same techniques that Stone Age people used. He also wants to show that every generation has to relearn and reteach these skills; they are fragile and could disappear if one generation did not actively reconstruct them. The essay traces chronologically the passage of skills through generations. The first section fills in the passage of the hammer from Sanders's grandfather to his father to him. The second section moves to his passing the hammer to his son and daughter. Thus the essay breaks out of the limitations of death that Sanders faced in the opening. Though his father died, though he was furious and even thought of maiming himself (cutting off his thumb) in his anger and grief, he continued after his death to pass on the skills his father taught him. The essay ends a few hours after it begins, but we can place those hours in a long chain stretching back through time and into the future and see that there has been no real interruption.

## Connections to Other Essays

In "Notes of a Native Son," James Baldwin (page 156) also writes about what he inherited from his father. Baldwin has great difficulty accepting his inheritance because it is not an inheritance of a stable world in which everything is "square and true." Rather, Baldwin inherits a raging anger at a terribly unjust world and the ability and necessity to live with complete contradictions. Yet the two essays are structured very much the same way — as flashbacks from news of a father's death. Both essays show in their very structure the way that accumulated memories passed from generation to generation — in other words, culture — bridge and transcend the gaps created by the loss of individuals.

"A Tribute to My Father" by Barbara Seidel (page 454) shows another way for a writer to achieve the distance and control to write well about intimate, strongly emotional topics. Sanders puts his emotions into the edges of an essay about tools and thereby gains the distance to convey those emotions very powerfully. Seidel writes in the third person, adopting a point of view not her own, to similarly gain distance. We might be tempted to say that these writers reduce their subjectivity by writing in these indirect ways, but it seems more accurate to say that they actually gain greater access to their own emotions, their own subjectivity, and acquire an external view that allows them to bring uninvolved readers to share those emotions.

## JOHN E. MASON, JR., "Shared Birthdays," page 388

## Teaching Strategies

Mason's assignment was to describe a person in his or her setting. Ostensibly Mason's purpose was to describe a beloved second-grade teacher, Mrs. Sullivan, whose funeral he had decided to attend on a moment's impulse. However, the essay is less a description or recollection of Mrs. Sullivan and more a journey in narrative form back to events from the writer's youth. The road he travels to the funeral provides the organizing principle for the essay, each spot passed brings forward a memory of a place or local celebrity that has played some role in his life. Mason recounts the trip itself in detail so that even while our attention is drawn to features along the way, we never lose sight of the narrator who is hurrying to the funeral.

Mason's remembrance takes him to the treasured spots to childhood, the playground, the drive-in movie; it includes friends, introduced briefly, and store owners, in anecdotes that suggest what it was like growing up in a small town in Connecticut. (In this respect it shares features of Ravenel Curry's essay "A Small Town" in *Student Writers at Work,* second edition.) Each pause is developed almost as if readers were permitted to enter the character's mind and see the past as he does, drawing little distinction between memories. The two most prominent vignettes deal with old girlfriends, a bit overextended but undoubtedly hard to put aside. The fact of Mrs. Sullivan's funeral reappears intermittently, giving a secondary organizing principle to the essay. Only when Mason is considering his old teacher does he exhibit doubt or indecision. His inability to remember her face troubles him. As the portrait of Mrs. Sullivan begins to fill in, we learn that Mason shared a birthdate with her, a memory that assumes special significance. The funeral occupies the last two paragraphs of the essay, tying together some of the earlier themes — remembered kindness, a brief moment of glory — and ends with the real purpose for the paper, the journal itself: "He was happy, not only for having attended the funeral, but for having taken the back road, even if as usual he had waited until the last minute."

Attention should be drawn to the choice of point of view. Clearly the main character in the recollection is the writer himself. Yet Mason chooses the more anonymous stance of third-person observer. Although he does not explain his narrative choice, we sense that he employs the impersonal third person as a way to avoid deflecting attention from the subject. Students may notice the same device operating in the essay by Terry Burns. Perhaps overemphasis on achieving a neutral role has created a different problem — that of the sense of a voice being thrown like a ventriloquist's, at once artificial and baffling. This is particularly true in paragraph 5 where readers may have to sort pronoun references: "He slowed down for the newly installed light in front of Elmore's. Although it was not actually Elmore's since a glass company bought it out, he still insisted on calling it Elmore's. In the same way he called Jerry Z's Restaurant, Dell's, after its original owners."

The narration takes a rambling form at times, one memory prompting another; while it creates a full picture of life in that small town, it sometimes lacks focus. But this is always a problem for student writers — how much detail is enough, how little is too little. Good description is a balancing act: knowing what it takes to tip readers over or what we need to keep us on the wire requires practice and editing.

## Further Suggestions for Reading, Writing, and Discussion

Other essays that offer examples of descriptive detail are Heather Ashley's "Leaving Vacita" (page 29), Ann Louise Field's "The Sound of Angels" (page 147), Patrick Kinder Lewis's "Five Minutes North of Redding" (page 320) Paula Sisler's "The Water Lily" (page 496). For another description of small-town life, students might compare William G. Hill's "Returning Home" (page 233).

A short exercise in description is to have students share a memory of a childhood friend. Chances are the memories will concern themselves with subjects similar to those Mason recalls, so it is important to have students think of ways to make the memory a personal portrait, one that draws on their unique ability to sketch. Treat the portrait as if it were literally a picture or photograph. Have students decide whether they want to place the subject in the foreground or background; how they want to light the subject; and whether the subject should be still or moving. Some discussion of these options may encourage students to think of other distinctions. This is good for an in-class writing assignment that can easily be shared with a writing response group or writing partner on the day it is written. If students have pictures of friends they have described it might be interesting to share those later and compare the written and photographic versions. Discourage the statistical portrait — "my friend is six feet tall and weighs two hundred pounds."

## Instructor's Comments: *Patricia Lynch, Central Connecticut State University*

Every student's work is unique; every student's work can be improved. Poor grammar and spelling mean problems and should be worked on, but the quality of the writing can nonetheless be powerful. Of course, revisions of the technical errors will result in really good work on all fronts.

Teachers should remember that there were great writers who had poor spelling and uncertain grammar but overcame these obstacles and that other literati, such as Joyce, virtually threw punctuation out! Perhaps some teachers concentrate too much on the formalities of writing. In Ireland [where Lynch now teaches], I feel that there is more cognizance given to literary merit than in the United States. There, too, there is a place for the vigorous idioms of speech that can sometimes be usefully incorporated into certain kinds of writing.

**VIRGINIA WOOLF,** "The Death of the Moth," page 397

## Teaching Strategies

Some instructors might, with good reason, regard this as an essay that they do not want their students to imitate, because students might take it as justifying their use of wildly broad generalizations. Most teachers of writing would prefer that their students do not write sentences about "life" in general, as Woolf does in paragraph 3. This essay can serve rather to demonstrate how hard a writer must work to ground abstract speculations in concrete detail.

The basic way Woolf keeps her readers from being lost in the fog of abstraction is by describing a scene in detail. Woolf balances and intricately intertwines careful, even minute descriptions and extremely general thoughts. Consider Woolf's abstract comment in paragraph 2: "The possibilities of pleasure seemed that morning so enormous and so various that to have only a moth's part in life, and a day moth's at that, appeared a hard fate." We would have only a vague idea of what she means by "possibilities of pleasure" if she had not earlier described at length the plough "scoring the field," the "vigor" of the rolling fields, and the rooks keeping their "annual festivities," making us see the moth's "fluttering" against a background of thousands of things moving in rapid, broad sweeps. The phrase "possibilities of pleasure" seems to refer back to the possibilities that everything in the world has of moving happily and vigorously. In contrast to these possibilities, the moth's pleasure is limited because its range of motion is limited. Woolf has set up a vivid and concrete image to represent the vague "possibilities of pleasure."

Consider Woolf's comments on "life" in paragraph 3. She makes statements so broad and abstract as to be almost meaningless: "One is apt to forget all about life" and "one could not get over the strangeness of it [life]." But she does not simply make these flat statements. First she gives us a picture of "life": "It was as if someone had taken a tiny bead of pure life and decking it as lightly as possible with down and feathers, had set it dancing and zigzagging to show us the true nature of life." She is, of course, describing the moth — and her description makes the moth seem very strange. For one thing, she is factually incorrect, creating a moth that never existed anywhere — one with down and feathers. Further, she makes us think that inside the actual moth there is a "bead" of life that is then decked out with all the gaudy decorations of moth wings. This "bead" provides a concrete image for that general term "life" that she wants to talk about. We can imagine "beads" of life inside ourselves. When Woolf then turns to her extreme generalizations, we have this precise, funny, absurd image to hold on to. And in her general statements, she uses words that also create strange, funny images: "One is apt to forget all about life, seeing it humped and bossed and garnished and cumbered so that it has to move with the greatest circumspection and dignity." This sentence probably defies literal explanation, but she has turned "life" into a rather amusing kind of person — one who perhaps has so many clothes and such tight corsets on that she cannot move. The word "garnished" recalls "decking" the bead of life: we get a sense that if only life were "naked," it would be free to move in those huge broad sweeps that are so pleasurable; but unfortunately "life" has been covered over and hemmed in. We can see that Woolf is commenting not merely on "life" in general but quite specifically on British lifestyles — all tightly wrapped in their proper manners.

The point of doing such a detailed analysis is to show how Woolf turns the kind of ridiculously general statements that teachers are forever trying to eliminate into humorous, vivid sentences. The overall structure of this piece, its use of a short narrative frame to organize her thoughts, is crucial: the narrative grounds the abstract thoughts. If students can see the complex relationships between the particular words in her abstract sentences and the particular events and scenes in her little narrative, they will see how Woolf makes abstractions into emotionally effective sentences.

This essay is particularly appropriate for detailed examination. Consider the next-to-last sentence: Woolf speaks of the moth lying "most decently and uncomplainingly composed." The word "composed" has several meanings and perhaps reveals the purpose of this whole essay: to bring herself to believe that the world is composed — orderly — so that she can remain composed — calm — as she tries to compose words to speak about her intense reactions to death. This whole essay puts a "decent" surface over the indecencies of mass slaughter and accidental deaths that repeatedly disrupted Virginia Woolf's life (she obliquely refers to those indecencies in the last paragraph when she says that death has "submerged an entire city, not merely a city, but masses of human beings").

## Connections to Other Essays

Woolf's essay can be paired with Annie Dillard's essay on the same subject ("Death of a Moth," page 330) for discussions of how writers differ in their approaches to a topic. Margot Harrison compares Woolf's and Dillard's essays in her critical analysis "Creative Transfiguration from the Death of a Moth" (page 201). For notes on using all three of these essays in an assignment sequence, see the instructor's manual entry on Annie Dillard, "Death of a Moth."

## AN-THU QUANG NGUYEN, "Tái Con," page 402

### Teaching Strategies

Nguyen's essay was a complex response to the connections developing between two earlier essays she had written on two separate topics:

(I):
HOME . . . "a place of the mind" variously, for you, as — (a) the point you want to return to: destiny as origin, how we renew ourselves by recall, by reminding ourselves, or by becoming who we were while watching others go through (Agee, *A Death in the Family*) what we have already undergone, or (b) the center you write from ("where you're coming from"): the private "inner space" (Erikson on Freud, *Identity, Youth, and Crisis*) where, composed, you are always composing, or (c) the building you inhabit (House, dorm, apt....), the lifestyle of its space and architecture (as Agee on Gudger's, *Let Us Now*; McPhee on Fred Brown's, *The Pine Barrens*; Defoe on Crusoe's stockade; Didion on mansions, "Seacoasts of Despair").

(II):
ANOTHER LANGUAGE, ANOTHER SELF . . . Many of you have spent your early years, at home or school, in a language other than English and a culture other than American. Explore whatever aspects of this "self" in another language, another life have entered into who you are becoming now.

Nguyen's approach to the first topic was to test the nature of memory, "to define clearly my memories which had been turning about so vaguely in my mind beforehand and compare them with my parents'. We'd also been studying about memory in my psychology class so I wondered about memories and their distortion." The essay on "home", however, is as much about the process of remembering as it is the memory itself. The writer begins with the imperfectly recalled sensations that the experience leaves with her:

> I start from these senses, then add the physical details later, the opposite way in which a child will color in his coloring book. For me the sensations are my colors. They are vague, moving, indistinct, until the details are drawn about them, forming the defining outline, the shape of my story. I begin thus with the colors of my memories, because I *cannot* lose the senses, even when I want to forget. They stay with me: the shrills, the darkness, a descending sky. A thunderstorm.

Because this is an essay about the act of remembering, it calls for intense concentration and cooperation from readers. Shifts in speakers, in time frames, in language, in places, ask readers to actively assist in the construction of the experience. Information, the diverse tongues of the author's childhood, fleshed out in successive monologues, must be fitted together in jigsaw fashion. We read backward and forward, coming to understand the event as if we are one of the actors.

The various patterns are established in the first monologue. We must deal in the first section with three viewpoints — the father's, the mother's, the author's; two shifts in time — April 1968 and 1975; and three places — Saigon, Tân Sồn Nhất, the airplane. December 1985 marks the time of the remembering but not the events themselves. The mother and the author repeat the information established in the father's monologue, adding their own details and emotional contexts so that we understand events more fully with each succeeding speaker. This narrative structure is important to discuss with students. Jo Goodwin Parker's essay "What Is Poverty?" (page 555) uses a single monologue. But she might easily have chosen to write that essay by adding monologues for other speakers — the children, the husband who left, the person to whom she appears to be speaking — to give us a different sense of her experience.

The monologues are not perfect copies of each other. We must guess that the mother sewed the backpack in 1975 at Tân Sồn Nhất. We must also follow Nguyen's impressions carefully to understand the bombing, the transition in the van, the flashback to the conversations between the sisters. We almost have a sense that the essay has ended when the writer returns us to 1985 with the conversation about America's role in Vietnam.

The second section might easily stand on its own, as it once did as her essay on "Another Language, Another Self," for it is less about the events that drove the family from Vietnam and more about the ways in which Nguyen struggles with her heritage. In this section, the narrator now speaks alone; she is older; she is concerned not with what has happened but with how she encounters the cultures and languages of her three worlds. Class discussion might center on the ways in which the second section takes up other issues and offers a different narrative stance. Again it is important to point out the rich opportunities writers have to explore multiple aspects of their experience. We are almost sorry when the essay ends, so intimately have we come to know "Tâi Con."

One final point — the title itself is not explicitly explained: we must guess at its meaning from a bit of dialogue about Nguyen's performance of traditional songs before her relatives: "They listen to the lilting, wrongly stressed and accented rhythms coming from my throat. 'Tâi con!' In their laughing eyes, I am 'the little French kid' " (paragraph 66).

## Further Suggestions for Reading, Writing, and Discussion

Nguyen's essay offers students an opportunity to explore monologues and dialogues. Any writing assignment that focuses on recollection might lend itself easily to this form. One way to stimulate students' recall might be to ask them to write a monologue from the point of view of a small child and then a dialogue from the viewpoint of adults. Using these dramatic forms as the introduction, students might then continue the narration in either first person, as Nguyen does, or third person, incorporating information generated from the earlier writings.

## Instructor's Comments: *George S. Fayen, Yale University*

Often, in writing, the need for shape must constrain energies that could have found wider, fuller expression — the other essay on the same subject we didn't write, with a different angle and foreground, or the next chapter in a story which for the moment had to end here and now. It was in this spirit one day, in class discussion, that we found ourselves seeking an afterlife for our exiled choices.

"Tâi Con" is an instance, then, not simply of two separate essays joined but more of the discovery, after the first essay, that it looked ahead to another — and that only in their relationship could the first essay be fulfilled. For An-Thu the "place of memories" could have stood alone as statement but not as an experience to be commemorated in isolation. What still remained for her came out in the next essay, "Another Language, Another Self" and in her beginning anew in "Tâi Con" ("My friend . . . I need to go back"), and especially in its powerful last paragraph, in which she goes beyond the content of memory to make the act of writing re-create its very processes, the way we are led back through "certain clues" into reliving the original feel of the experience and its impact on the senses. So it is not a shape which finally emerges in the essay but a presence: the "gigantic regal tree" in their Saigon garden and the "pungent smell of its blossoms" can recall an afternoon when she and her mother heard, beyond the words, suffering in a woman's song.

## MAXINE HONG KINGSTON, "The Woman Warrior," page 417

### Teaching Strategies

Maxine Hong Kingston's essay has a structure similar to An-Thu Quang Nguyen's. Kingston shows us a slightly different way to write an essay made of disparate pieces and a slightly different reason for writing such an essay. She uses much smaller pieces than Nguyen and does not use white space to separate them: her scenes blend together. She is trying to express the experience of living a fragmented life. She, too, is writing about the confusion she feels from having lived in two different cultures, but she has not moved from one to another; she has simply grown up always surrounded by both Chinese and American traditions. As she says at the end of this chapter, "I have so many words — 'chink' words and 'gook' words too — that they do not fit on my skin." She gives us the experience of having words flung at us from all directions, being constantly interrupted, being unable to follow one line of thought to the end.

Kingston writes her essay for a different reason than Nguyen, and her reason also contributes to the way she organizes her essay. She is angry at almost all those words that are flung at her because they are sexist, racist, or simply cruel. Her anger provides a way to connect her scenes: she arranges a sequence of scenes that all illustrate the same point. At first the scenes all show sexism directed at her; then they show racism directed at others; then she includes several incidents of the mistreatment of her relatives in Communist China. In this chapter, she is not so much telling a tale as collecting many examples of injustice that have touched her life. Her chapter could actually be rewritten as a fairly straightforward essay, with topic sentences. For example, she could start with "I have experienced sexism in my family" and then go on to give the examples that fill the first twenty-six paragraphs. But that structure would create the feeling that she was in control of the argument. Instead, she wants to bring us to experience the feeling of frustration and entrapment that constantly repeated sexist comments cause a young woman, so she makes her examples into voices harping at her, interrupting her, frustrating her. Kingston shows how to write a powerful essay revealing and protesting against the contradictory and immoral voices in our lives.

Kingston threads together all the disparate little scenes in her essay by using a few motifs. References to swords and birds run throughout this chapter (birds in paragraphs 5, 26, 39, 40, 42, 43; swords in paragraphs 25, 35, 38, 44, 46, 47). Birds and swords are elements from the traditional tale of the woman warrior. Kingston's repeated use of these motifs makes us feel tradition winding around all the events of her life. Each time one of these elements appears, it takes a slightly different form and carries a slightly different meaning. Birds first appear as an insult — girls are compared to cowbirds. But this insult turns around when Kingston speaks of looking for a bird to guide her to triumph over the injustice around her. In the tale of her relatives in China, trying to eat birds to stave off starvation leads to their own death, and Kingston says, "birds tricked us" (paragraph 43). Kingston thus seems ambivalent about tradition — she wants to rely on it, to trust it, but it does not seem to work in the modern world.

Swords at first seem also to suggest that tradition is worthless; she can talk about using swords to get revenge for the injustices in her life, but such talk seems merely empty fantasy. However, in the last paragraph, Kingston reverses all the hopelessness in the essay by discovering that she does have the power to get revenge. She does not need a physical sword to behead people, because the "ideographs for *revenge* are 'report a crime' and 'report to five families.' The reporting is the vengeance — not the beheading, not the gutting, but the words."

She definitely does have words — too many, she says in the last sentence. Her power as a writer makes her a swordswoman and reverses all the failures of the legends in her life. This book is an act of violence in words revenging all the violence done to her through words. She finds a way that traditional magic still works.

### Connections to Other Essays

Several other essays deal with the experience of ethnic minorities or immigrants. Richard Rodriguez in "Hunger of Memory" (page 478) discusses growing up in two cultures, as Kingston does, but Rodriguez feels that he has left his minority culture behind and become a mainstream American. James Seilsopour in "I Forgot the Words to the National Anthem" (page 472) discusses the disorienting experience of admiring America while living in Iran and then moving to the United States and discovering that he is treated as a despicable alien, almost an enemy. Seilsopour and Rodriguez use sudden jumps from one scene to another, as Kingston does, to re-create the jarring experience of moving from one culture to another.

James Baldwin in "Notes of a Native Son" (page 156) writes of his discovery that blacks are hated in America, a discovery that is shocking because he felt comfortable as a child in the company of whites. Doris Lessing in "The Old Chief Mshlanga" (page 522) writes from the opposite experience: discovering that whites are a hated minority in Africa. Both of these writers, like Kingston, explore the myths they had to escape to recognize the real character of race relations. David Landmann in "The House" (page 309) discusses the way the middle class tries to ignore and render invisible a black man, a theme that Baldwin also explores. Most of these writers end up accusing the ruling-class whites of racism and injustice. Doris Lessing presents an unusual version of this accusation because the ruling class in her story is the minority to which she belongs: thus guilt mixes with her anger. Richard Rodriguez presents a striking contrast, arguing that minority members must not try to make public use of their own cultural style and their own language as they try to succeed in America — they must join the dominant culture if they are to succeed. Rodriguez regards it as a subtle form of racism to always view a person of a particular ethnic background as a "minority."

Kingston parallels racism and sexism as forms of oppression in her essay. Francis Dana Barker Gage in "Sojourner Truth: And A'n't I a Woman?" (page 315) and Alice Walker in "A Letter of the Times" (page 266) also intertwine discussions of sexism and racism.

**ALLISON ROLLS,** "Lady Diana: He Married the Wrong Woman," page 426

The standard comparison and contrast paper takes on added charm in the hands of Allison Rolls, whose comic essay is a spirited response to excessive media coverage of a public event. Rolls's piece began when she asked herself a healthy question: "What's Diana got that I ain't got?" Students may enjoy applying that inquiry to their favorite idol, thus ensuring some lively papers in this sometimes artificial mode.

Rolls's tone is exactly right. She combines, with ease, the phrasing of an aristocratic British narrator with the blunt voice of injured American vanity. For example, when she refers to Diana's pregnancy, she is at her drollest: "to simply 'lie still and think of England,' as Diana certainly did on her wedding night, displays to me a certain lack of character, and to feel that one's role in life . . . should be as a baby factory seems a sadly outmoded outlook."

The scope of her attack is also comically effective. Not content to lament the loss of Charles, Rolls takes swipes at the Queen, at Prince Andrew, and at the war in the Falklands. The portrait that emerges of the writer, a young woman with high SAT scores who has no "hordes of hungry relatives," who sews her own clothes, who knows how to bring thrift to the royal budget, is a splendidly funny contrast to what she calls the "Barbie-doll" charms of Lady Diana. She ends on a humorous but aggrieved note: "I am quite positive that he, his country, and the future history books will be all the more bored for it."

**Further Suggestions for Reading, Writing, and Discussion**

Comparison and contrast assignments often develop into forced or artificial explorations of an idea. An interesting point about a number of the essays in the text is that, although they contain comparisons and contrasts, the larger purpose behind the various pieces suggests that this device alone is not sufficient to express the writer's intentions. For example, Karen L. Kramer turns a comparison and contrast paper into a parody of musicians in "The Little Drummer Boys" (page 292). Rolls, in attempting a satire, discovers quite naturally that a comparison and contrast format will work the comic point effectively. Research papers often include the device. An examination of readings in conventional rhetoric will reveal that although a piece may fall generally into the category, the writer may not have intended to write such an essay.

It may be enlightening for students to examine any of their essays for sections that might have been more clearly defined had they incorporated the device as part of the overall essay. This allows them to see comparison as one strategy, not as the overriding purpose in writing descriptions or explanations.

**Instructor's Comments: *Nancy A. Sours, San Francisco State University***

I don't have any grand theories about teaching composition, but I do believe that reading conveys not only style and fluency, but also a sense that ideas and opinions *matter.*

**ALICE KAHN,** "Pianotherapy: Primal Pop," page 433

**Teaching Strategies**

Alice Kahn creates irony by repeatedly shifting her portrayal of her musical efforts so that we cannot be certain whether she views her singing as silly or admirable. She begins her essay as Allison Rolls does, by describing herself as foolishly holding on to fantasies and feeling silly when she acts them out. She seems to be admitting an embarrassing egotism; she is childishly angry at the "unjust world" that gave her a lousy voice, but she will sing out anyway. Then Kahn changes tone and makes us think that her initial presentation of herself was just an ironic pose, a way of being modest before claiming great powers for her music. She leads us to a new view of her music by telling us that as a child music was her "only friend" when her parents were fighting. She could "charm" them by "banging the ivories"; this use of music as a way out of an "unjust" world does not seem egotistical at all. When she tells how her music served to end drug nightmares at the Berkeley Free Clinic, we begin to believe that even embarrassingly bad music can save the soul.

Just when Kahn has convinced us that her music has a serious, even noble purpose, she drops in the most embarrassing scene of all — chasing the mailman away by trying to "give him a song and dance for Christmas." She leaves us uncertain whether we should admire her music or be appalled. The essay ends with a sentence that could have several meanings and so teeters on a fine ironic edge between the two views of her music. She says the goal of her singing has always been "to make the world go away." The statement is at first absurd: she seems to say she has been playing music to *purposely* drive people away. But then we realize that she could be serious in two opposite ways: she could be saying she plays to find some peace in any angry, nightmarish world; or she could be saying she wants to be alone because she is terribly embarrassed at her foolishness.

Many of Kahn's sentences are like that last line, delicately balanced between contrary possible meanings. Consider the line in paragraph 9, "sometimes I'm Frankie singing 'Why Do Fools Fall in Love?' so sweetly and happily that you'd swear the whole world was fourteen years old." Is it good or bad to imagine that the whole world is fourteen years old? Is the real question asked by her song "Why do fools sing out loud?" Similarly, in the first paragraph, she interrupts her fantasy of dressing in a fox wrap with the parenthetical comment "fake! fake animal fur!" She seems to be simply reminding us that she is not so carried away by her fantasy that she forgets current issues. Or is she emphasizing the word "fake" to brand herself a fake?

To develop a feel for irony, students might practice writing single sentences or short paragraphs that balance contrary attitudes. Some students will have an affinity for irony, and others will prefer writing sincerely. Playing with irony, they can begin to discover their own voices.

## Connections to Other Essays

Alice Kahn's essay, like Allison Rolls's, leaves us in doubt whether the writer is being sincere or ironic. To help students see the range of possible voices that writers can use, from sincere to ironic, you might group this unit with two others — the Beverly Dipo/Oliver Sacks unit and the Ha Song Hi/Mark Twain unit. Dipo and Sacks try very hard to be sincere, to win their readers' trust. Hi and Twain carry the ironic pose very far, creating identities for narrators that are patently false and unbelievable — Hi's narrator is an insect from another planet; Twain's is an angel. These three units define a continuum of writer's voices from sincere to ironic:

*Sincere:* Dipo/Sacks
*Playfully ironic* — uncertain whether to believe the speaker or not: Rolls/Kahn
*Obviously ironic* and unbelievable: Hi/Twain

All of these six essays are written in the first-person point of view and so they can easily be compared. The students can discuss the difference between the narrator, the "I" in the essay, and the author. Are any of these writers simply "being themselves" as they write? Does an author have to be just as artificial and work just as hard to create the impression that he or she is being honest and sincere (as Dipo and Sacks do) as to create an ironic pose?

## JILL A. SAVITT, "Decisions," page 437

### Teaching Strategies

Jill Savitt's essay evolved out of an assignment, based on Richard Rodriguez's *Hunger of Memory,* asking students to explain "the way we go about making decisions." Referring to a newspaper article written for the *Miami Herald,* Savitt explains, "I wrote my Bedford essay to discover why I wrote about the event which sparked it." Just as her classmate An-Thu Quang Nguyen wrote to clarify her emotions about a crucial event, Savitt uses her essay to explore the conflicting feelings that grew out of her role as a cub reporter for the newspaper. In part the essay is about what happened, but more important it is a record of the author's writing about the writing. As such it is almost like a double-entry journal in which both the experience and the interpretation are recorded at the same time.

The form itself became a struggle: "How do I write about thoughts occurring simultaneously? Manipulate the layout. At one point I trashed this idea . . . , thinking if I had the right words I could say what I meant. I didn't need to play with design. Words alone, if they are the best words, would convey the conflict. Manipulate words, not layout. But then I thought, 'What would *The Sound and the Fury* be without the italicized parts?' " Savitt's decision seems to grow out of her training as a journalist. She chooses side-by-side columns to report her dual feelings. While she has prepared readers in the more straightforward narration at the beginning for the quandary she poses when she introduces the columns, she does not explain the shift in narrative form. Readers must fill in the blank. We must read the columns carefully to discover her purpose. Clearly this is a fine opportunity for students to examine two texts emerging simultaneously, which is a considerably different task than comparing sequential drafts. We seem to be almost participants rather than spectators in an internal debate: we hear the writer's needs arguing against the victim's needs. We want to know the outcome. As Savitt concludes: "I wrote the paper in the form of a decision and I knew I had finished when, upon rereading, I wanted to flip the pages to know what I had decided."

Savitt has done an excellent job of balancing the two narrative strategies of the essay, offering a bit of recitative of the original debate later in the essay. She laces the narrative with a good deal of dialogue, which again allows readers to understand the pressures surrounding her decision. The quarrels with the editors dramatize the strength of her decision and the pleasure we later feel when, with the permission of Carol and her family, she finally gets her byline honorably.

This is Jill Savitt's article, which appeared on page 1 of the *Miami Herald* on April 17, 1986. The names have been changed.

### SCARED DAUGHTER
### Teen's FBI father survived
### — but it was a nightmare

Carol Sanders, who will be 17 on Friday, was born into an FBI family. A photo of her father shaking hands with bureau director William Webster decorates a wall in her South Dade home.

Last Friday, though, Carol learned that being the daughter of FBI Special Agent James Sanders can involve fear, anxiety and heartache — as well as pride.

As Carol sat in her fourth-period class at Palmetto Senior High School, a nightmare slowly, dreadfully unfolded.

Shirley Yaskin's journalism class was interrupted by two students bringing news: There had been a deadly shoot-out just a few blocks away. Yaskin warned her class to avoid the area around Southwest 124th Street and 82nd Avenue during the lunch break.

"I heard people talking," said Carol, a senior, at her home this week. "I just heard pieces of a conversation — two agents were killed. I looked up and said, 'What? What? What happened?'

"I immediately got nervous. I said, 'My dad, that's my dad's case.' So I thought I'd call the office to see if everything was OK."

She used the phone in the journalism classroom to contact her father's office.

"No one wanted to tell me the news," Carol said. "They connected me to a whole bunch of people. I said, 'This is Carol Sanders. May I speak to James Sanders please?'

" 'Oh,' they said, 'what do you want?'

"I said I wanted to speak to him. They got nervous. . . . Finally some lady got on, and I said, 'Where's my father?'

"She said, 'I know you're upset. Your father's OK. He's in the hospital; we're sending an agent to come get you.'

"At that point, I figured they just weren't telling me. I thought he was dead and they didn't want to tell me over the phone."

As she ran down a school hallway to meet the agent, she thought, "My God, this isn't happening to me. This only happens in movies," she said.

"The thought of my father's life being in danger never even occurred to me. I know his job is dangerous and I know the people he works with are dangerous people. You never feel it can happen to you."

The agent took her to Baptist Hospital, where her father, a 19-year FBI veteran, received emergency treatment for a chest wound and hand injuries suffered in a gun battle with two armored-car and bank robbers, William Matix and Michael Lee Platt.

The robbers and two FBI special agents, Benjamin Grogan and Gerald Dove, were killed. Sanders and four other agents were wounded.

The first family member to see James Sanders, Carol watched her father being wheeled into an X-ray room on a gurney.

Her mother, Elizabeth Sanders, was next to arrive. Later, Carol's 13-year-old sister, Kathleen, and an aunt arrived at the hospital.

"I saw him in really bad shape — all bloody and everything. That was scary," Carol said. "It was scary — seeing my big, strong dad helpless. It was totally different than I'd ever seen him. I felt relief, but love, because he was there and everything was OK.

"When I think about what could have happened . . . my dad could easily have been Mr. Grogan or Mr. Dove. I just keep saying to myself, he's so lucky. We're so lucky."

Carol's mother said that as her husband left home Friday morning she intuitively felt there would be a break in the case.

"For some reason, just because he was going out Friday — I mean he had such a personal vendetta against these people because they were so bad," Mrs. Sanders said.

"It wasn't doom; it was just realizing that if and when they did catch up with these two that probably something would happen," said Mrs. Sanders, who worked for eight years as a secretary for the FBI.

As Carol spoke Tuesday afternoon, she sat comfortably on the living room couch. No lights were on. Carol's blond, almost white, hair and pink sweater stood out in the shadows of the earth-tone room.

On a table rested two remote-control units — for one television. "We're all too lazy to get up and change the channel," Carol said. "Anyway, one's broken and Dad's not home to fix it."

The table's centerpiece was a fresh flower arrangement. More flowers, along with fruit baskets and gifts, ringed the room. One gift card was signed by *Miami Vice* star Don Johnson. Another was from the parents of Beth Kenyon, a victim of sex-killer Christopher Wilder. James Sanders worked on the Wilder investigation.

In the immediate aftermath of Friday's shootings, Carol said, "It was crazy" — but now she can reflect on and talk about what happened.

"On Friday I felt relief, pure relief," she said. "On Saturday it was grief. It was a total change. On Friday, I was happy for him just to be alive. And then Saturday I realized what it would do to him mentally. My father had guilt even though it wasn't his fault. Those were his friends."

Carol said her father had never let the danger and frustrations of his job interfere with his family life.

"Sometimes I think my dad and the FBI agent are two different people. I have so much respect for him now. I didn't realize it was so scary," she said.

"He is funny, so funny. Everybody loves him. When we got all the calls and all the people writing and visiting, I respected him so much because of how I saw other people respected him," she said.

Carol remembers her father's playful antics at her birthday party when she was in the eighth grade. "He came out on the patio in a blond curly wig and a pink tutu — anything to embarrass me," she said.

"I have so much more respect now for him because I realize the great deal of pressure, and what responsibilities he has on his mind all the time. You can't pack that up at 5 o'clock and go home," Carol said.

"He was the supervisor of the case, and he was really hurt about the two other agents. They were his friends and his co-workers.

"The really strange thing is that this guy, Matix, lives nine blocks away. My dad was after him for so long, chasing him all around town, and he probably passed him on his jog," Carol said.

Mrs. Sanders said her husband's decision to set up a stakeout Friday for Matix and Platt was "nothing more than just an educated hunch on his part.

"But, knowing how bad they were, I knew it was possible, just possible they could find them — never dreaming this could happen."

While recuperating from his wounds, Special Agent Sanders has described to his family the emotional trauma of being shot.

"He told me that he was lying there on the ground thinking he was paralyzed or dead," Carol said. "He didn't think he had a chance. He said all he could think about was me, my mom and my sister."

Carol's perception of her father's profession has changed.

"At school, people have always said, 'Wow, oh wow.' And I always responded, 'It's no big deal.' But it is a big deal and I never realized what was really involved."

## Further Suggestions for Reading, Writing, and Discussion

Terry L. Burns's assignment that resulted in "The Blanket Party" (page 76) called for a narrative role in which the writer was an observer, not a participant, but must also include his reactions. Savitt's essay seems to do almost the opposite. She must be an observer and a participant at the same time. The two essays provide a valuable opportunity for discussing values and decisions and for exploring in writing the duality of roles that arises in a decision-making process. Students might consider some narrative strategies — multiple points of view in the form of monologues such as An-Thu Quang Nguyen (page 402) uses or Faulkner's representation of thought by the use of italics. Students might be asked to determine how many different methods writers use to dramatize internal debate.

## Instructor's Comments: *George S. Fayen, Yale University*

The double-column device of Jill Savitt's "Decisions" is clearly effective drama. It compels us in the reading, as it did her in the writing, to undergo the conflict in all its unresolved immediacy.

Less obvious, though, are the implications. What does her use of this device as a writer really say about herself in the situation? To set out a dilemma in two newspaper columns: Is this the reporter's self-regard that is competing with her personal self-respect? in the very form of fame under a byline on the front page? or is its formal discipline already a sign of the scrupulous care that was to prevail in her conscience?

Either way, this essay shows that layout and visual arrangements can themselves be as eloquent as the syntax of a sentence. It puts to us the issues, problems, questions that are traditionally reserved for the novelist — and demonstrates that literary techniques can truthfully illuminate materials conventionally reserved for neutral exposition. In these certainties, through its professional skill, "Decisions" reminds us that journalism can be an art.

**NORA EPHRON,** "The Boston Photographs," page 447

### Teaching Strategies

Nora Ephron might not seem to use the same device that Savitt does, since Ephron does not "dramatize" her dilemma in the sense of creating a scene with characters. Our decision to use Ephron's essay does stretch what it means to "dramatize" an issue. But Ephron's essay is so close to Savitt's in structure as well as in topic that we felt it instructive to match the two. The two essays demonstrate how subtle the distinction is between an essay written as a narrative and an essay written "as an essay." Ephron and Savitt both build suspense by making readers listen to many conflicting and compelling voices, and both writers delay to the very end telling us what they think is the "right" solution to the issue the voices are discussing. Ephron does not begin her essay with a "thesis" but rather with a quote that puts us inside the mind of the photographer, the man actually at the scene, the man faced with the dilemma, just as Savitt begins her essay with an internal monologue. We feel a part of the scene before we have to face the difficult issue. Ephron, like Savitt, provides only the briefest descriptions of the "characters" she is quoting and only a short sketch of the setting.

About half of Ephron's essay consists of quotations, and she lets two persons speak at some length — the photographer, Stanley Forman (in the first paragraph), and Charles Seib, an editor (in paragraphs 6–9). Ephron herself emerges as a character, speaking directly to us, in the last two paragraphs. Thus we have a sense of watching persons speaking directly to us, as if they were on a stage, telling us about a difficult dilemma that we do not know how to resolve. At the end, we see the dilemma solved through a decision made by the narrator. Ephron's essay works just as a dramatic scene would work, even though it is not overtly a scene. Ephron's final conclusion should provoke controversy in class. Would she be willing to print any pictures that are a part of life? Pictures of sexual perversions? What limits should be placed on pictures in newspapers and on television?

In paragraph 11, Ephron uses an argumentative strategy that is rather suspect — she refers to "the Nixon-Agnew years" and to "puritanism," making it seem as if anyone who is against printing the Boston photographs is a Nixonite and a Puritan. She gets very close to name-calling. Her logic is a bit loose in this paragraph as well. She parallels Nixon's argument that the press should not print "bad news" with the argument that the press should not print pictures of dead people. But it is easy to see that the press has a duty to print the "bad news" that Nixon disliked — the bad news about presidential crimes. It is not so easy to see that the press has any parallel duty to print pictures of dead people. Students might discuss whether this essay is intended to resolve difficult issues or to stimulate, to rile up, and ultimately to entertain readers.

### Connections to Other Essays

"The House" by David Landmann (page 309) also discusses what is left out of newspapers and out of most people's consciousness. A homeless man is as distasteful a subject for most writers as is death — and as difficult a subject to handle well.

**BARBARA SEIDEL,** "A Tribute to My Father," page 454

Seidel's assignment was to write a tribute to someone. She chose to deal with her father, knowing that to write honestly she must be "open and vulnerable." Moreover, she recognized "that if I worried about the reaction of my dad or other family members to whatever I would write, I would become too paralyzed with the attempt to please everybody else to write honestly."

Seidel decided to use a third-person point of view, a solution several other students have used to give distance to a subject that involved them intimately. Terry L. Burns in "The Blanket Party" (page 76) also chose the third-person narrator, which freed him from self-conscious statements and allowed him to speak plainly about an emotionally difficult subject. Students should note the opportunities that such a narrative stance affords them. In some cases as in John E. Mason, Jr.'s "Shared Birthdays" (page 388), for example, use of the third person may not entirely serve the writer's purpose, particularly if readers question the need for such distance. However, in the case of Seidel, the use of the third person affords her the opportunity to switch seamlessly between the stories of three generations, thus keeping the focus on the subject of her father.

One of the attributes of the essay is the ease with which Seidel moves back and forth between her grandparents' relationship to her father and that of her father to her brother and to her. We understand her father better because of the depth of the explanation. Seidel avoids a familiar temptation to see her father as a background to or an extension of his children. She encourages our understanding by allowing us to see him as the child of an errant father and an enduring mother, yet she never steps outside the narrative role to refer to them as her grandparents. This is, after all, her father's story.

The essay begins with a question about her father's devotion to his own father. The second paragraph provides a summary of her father's attributes, posed as a series of tensions between seemingly contradictory experience: "He has no textbook education, yet he possesses an abundance of common sense. He is not religious, yet he is a moral man, consistent in his values on a daily basis, not only on the Sabbath." Paragraph 3 gives us a brief insight into a satisfying marriage not touched on again until the end of the essay. Seidel's choice of detail is adroit. With simple references to "meat loaf served on the same day of each week" and her father's taste in clothes, she renders a solid portrait of a family man, conservative and comfortable. What the writer does not do is overwhelm us with details about any one period in his life.

The next three paragraphs switch back to his childhood. Seidel carefully mixes generalization with incident, making us understand both the events and the values that informed them. The scene of two small boys eating their one meager meal a day, a meal paid for in advance, tells worlds about her grandmother, just as the anecdote about her grandfather's lie explains the hardship her father endured. At no time does Seidel pause to pass judgment or try to make her father larger than life. The hidden Hershey bars and the compulsively neat approach to household tasks remind the reader that there are scars no amount of happiness will erase.

The next-to-last paragraph also offers an insight into a man who is not without his own feelings. His relationship with his son "who is one of the brief detours on his well-laid road map of life" again is simply illustrated by the ritual of the second phone call. Seidel does not dwell on her own relationship with her father as we might expect; rather she keeps the portrait focused by touching on all the people he loves, choosing to end the tribute with the scene of his new wife, visiting the grave of Seidel's mother. Again, she sidesteps a sentimental opportunity and returns the essay to its beginnings by reminding us of her father's devotion to those who have come under his protection.

The essay is well organized. Interconnections between paragraphs are clearly drawn and the focus never wavers. Seidel has created a universal sense in this tribute. Her father is not the sum of his experience or entirely a product of his setting. He is simply a good man, "the ultimate peacemaker."

The development of Seidel's essay is discussed at length in Chapter 1, "Revising Drafts."

## Further Suggestions for Reading, Writing, and Discussion

"Home Is Where the Heart Is" by Joanne Menter (*Student Writers at Work*, first edition) provides students with another example of a writer addressing a difficult subject in a detached yet intimate manner. Menter's first-person essay, which avoids sentimentality and cliché, is a tribute to her father's endurance during the terminal stages of an illness.

Shifts in point of view enable writers to discover their focus. A brief assignment that encourages students to include or omit information is to try a sketch of someone in their family from several viewpoints — their own, that of a parent, a grandparent, another sibling, a friend — and then combine the information developed by the sketches into one full portrait or tribute to the person. Students might try the third-person point of view or they may prefer to speak more directly in the first person, but the point of the exercise is to discover a balance between a tone that is personal yet dispassionate.

## Instructor's Comments: *Mary Ellen Byrne, Ocean County College*

Many of our students have years of negative attitudes, frustrations, and hostility toward writing when we encounter them. It is very difficult to overcome this background and to obtain great successes. Actually I try to maintain demanding standards while trying to encourage, but we lose many students along the way. The rewards may be few, but successes are possible with quality standards, discipline, and effort.

## CHRISTOPHER NOLAN, "Knife Used," page 461

### Teaching Strategies

Christopher Nolan's style might put some students off. Discussing the powerful emotions Nolan re-creates in this chapter before discussing the style might allow students to "get into" the book and then see how Nolan's style serves him in telling his tale. This chapter traces Nolan's (or Joseph Meehan's, as he calls himself) life from birth to winning a writing contest in his late teens. It is a classic tale of overcoming adversity and suffering to achieve a grand victory — very much like a tale of a great sports hero. Nolan begins with his intense childhood depression: "he had decided to choose death" even in the womb, "but fate decided otherwise." Almost everyone seems to agree with Nolan's suicidal feelings; even "history" says he is "better dead." Only his mother recognizes his undeveloped potential; she "tumbled to the hollyberries, green yet, but holding promise of burning in red given time." But to help him achieve his potential, his entire family must suffer, giving up their rural way of life to live in the big city of Dublin. Joseph himself must go through a painful, difficult process to finally break out of the shell of silence, but finally he succeeds. Nolan makes us share his "happy unbelievable bewilderment" when he can finally communicate in words.

Part of the appeal of Nolan's story is his honesty in portraying himself. He lets us see his egotism and his insecurity. The ending of the chapter brings together these contradictory feelings about himself. He imagines the entire city of Dublin "framing the story of Joseph Meehan," yet he still feels he is "a small fella" who does not understand why God performed a miracle for him. He needs to feel "close body contact" with his "comforter," God, through communion to feel secure. If we remember that Joseph needs "close body contact" with his "comforters," with others who help him, to do anything at all, we can see why his success is so fragile and insecure. In "close body contact" with God, he almost returns to the last time he was fully secure — in the womb that he had to be knifed out of at the beginning of his life (and at the beginning of this chapter). He presents himself as a remarkable combination of small child and brash adult.

The style of this chapter and of much of the book might be explained as Nolan's way to combine his childishness and his adult perceptions. He is at once playing joyfully with words and flinging challenges at the world that scorned and pitied him. To see how he compresses contrary attitudes, consider paragraph 34. He describes the sense of release that finally being able to write gives him, and yet at the same time mocks those who saved him: "Brain-damaged, he had for years clustered his words, certain that some Cyclops-visioned earthling would stumble on a scheme by which he could express hollyberried imaginings." He compares his saviors to Cyclops, implying that they are limited, one-eyed creatures who cannot see all the different ways he can see and who only "stumble" on a way to help him. He seems more irritated at the stupidity of scientists who took so long to figure out a way to help him than thankful over their final success.

In that same paragraph is a phrase that might serve as an example of Nolan's effective coinage of new terms. He says, "Writing became Joseph Meehan's Word-Wold." A wold is a hill; words have piled up, "clustered" in his brain until they have formed a hill that he now scampers across, scattering them about like fallen leaves, making phrases like "word-wold" that "normal" people have trouble pronouncing. The two words "word" and "wold" also seem to have other words hidden in them — "world" and "wood": words are his world, his woods, his hill, his playground, the place in which he is free from his body to move and grow. His mind is like a tree that grows in that wood/wold/world, making hollyberries that everyone can enjoy.

The combination of playfulness and contempt that Nolan expresses in this paragraph is one example of the duality of perspective that Nolan wants to share with us. He feels that he is a combination of several persons. In a later chapter, he creates a dream (quoted in the headnote) that symbolizes his feeling. He dreams that he is a window washer looking in at himself and asks, "How can Boyhood be in two places at once?" The question could apply to the whole book: how can Nolan make us aware that he is two — or more — persons at once? The odd device of giving himself a new name makes us continually aware of such splits in him. He is both the cripple who cannot move coherently and a brilliant writer who can leap about in words like an acrobat. He is both a young boy first playing with words and a writer aware of a long tradition. He is both a person needing constant support, physically and emotionally, and an egotist who feels superior to all about him.

This chapter provides an opportunity to discuss the risks and rewards of experimenting with words and sentences. To stimulate discussion of Nolan's style, you might have each student select one unusual sentence that seems to work very well and one that seems confusing or simply "bad." In class, students might help each other try to understand the confusing sentences and discuss what Nolan gains and loses by using the particular sentences they have selected.

**Connections to Other Essays**

Patricia Hampl's review of Nolan's book (page 212) provides a fine summary of the whole autobiography and may help students see this selection as one chapter of a long work. Hampl's review may also inhibit students from expressing their own opinions.

"Todd" by Celeste Barrus (page 47) also traces the intense drama of a child suffering and being helped by professionals. "Todd" is written from the first-person point of view of Todd's mother. Students might try to imagine how Nora, Christopher Nolan's mother, or Eva Fitzpatrick, his teacher, would have written the story of Nolan's life.

For some notes on other essays in this collection that present views of childhood, see the instructor's manual entry on Eudora Welty's "The Little Store."

**JAMES M. SEILSOPOUR,** "I Forgot the Words to the National Anthem," page 472

The absence of bitterness in Seilsopour's tone is explained by his purpose in writing the essay: "When people read my essay I want them to imagine themselves in my place for just a moment — then never think about it again. My essay originated from some poetry I had written. . . . The only problem I had was toning the paper down from an angry commentary to a straightforward personal essay."

Implicit in this essay is a comparison between the conventional concerns of an American teenager — rock-and-roll, cars, movie stars — and the cares forced on him by the disruption in Iran. Unaware at the beginning of his return to the United States of the differences between himself and his classmates, Seilsopour is forced to face the prejudice that the Iranian crisis prompted. What might easily have been a sermon or catalogue of injuries is instead a carefully controlled selection of moments that illustrate the family's humiliation.

Attention should be drawn to Seilsopour's method of achieving distance. Seilsopour has chosen the ordinary moments at home, in class, and at a supermarket to make his point. Each vignette is introduced briefly, but the main focus is on the event, which Seilsopour allows to stand for itself.

He does not moralize. We hear the various voices that have caused suffering, not only through Seilsopour's words but through the dialogue and exchanges that appear throughout the essay. The moment in the supermarket is a fine example of Seilsopour's instinct for selecting appropriate illustrations of his point. So too is the reference to the father staring blankly at the wall.

**Further Suggestions for Reading, Writing, and Discussion**

Some readings that present different aspects of bias are James Baldwin's essay "Stranger in the Village" and Nathaniel Hawthorne's short story "Gentle Boy." Langston Hughes's barroom philosopher, Jesse B. Semple, offers his version of prejudice in "That Word Black," taken from *Semple Takes a Wife.* An ironic view of the word "American" is provided in Ralph Linton's essay "One Hundred Per Cent American."

In his essay "Streets of Gold: The Myth of the Model Minority" (page 90), Curtis Chang notes the way in which bias, even when it seems to favor a group or individual, ultimately denies our real identity. Despite the different purpose of Seilsopour's essay, students might benefit from examining Chang's thesis in conjunction with Seilsopour's point.

**Instructor's Comments:** *William F. Hunt, Riverside City College*

I liked James Seilsopour. I often share my scribblings with my students, and I recall saying only two things to him: Don't tell me how I'm supposed to feel, and read a couple of Hemingway short stories if you have time.

I read his essay to the class, but most of my students were still hanging yellow ribbons here and there. James's voice is authentic and it is his. In fact, he told me he had been struggling for quite some time to get a new bumper sticker. I'm not sure how he managed to control his tone, his voice, his point of view, and so forth. I felt that it was a matter of life and death to him, very delicate stuff, so I grinned crookedly, was in a bit of a hurry, and told him I really didn't have time to listen to his stories, but that it was my job to read what he wrote. Oh, yes! I told him to write what he would, to forget the writing requirements for the course, and to write for publication. I don't have to tell you that his winning means a great deal to me.

## RICHARD RODRIGUEZ, "Hunger of Memory," page 478

### Teaching Strategies

Richard Rodriguez wants to disrupt the expectations readers bring to his autobiography, *Hunger of Memory,* so he has written a prologue full of sudden, unexplained transitions. He leaps from allusions to a Shakespeare play (Caliban is a character in *The Tempest*) to a fairy tale ("Once upon a time") to the language of social issues ("socially disadvantaged"). He constantly interrupts scenes he starts to describe, even interrupting his own sentences, leaving fragments and parenthetical comments scattered throughout his text. His opening makes his readers ask many questions and wonder what is going to come next. Most important, we cannot tell what kind of book this is going to be. Rodriguez knows that most people are going to expect that he will write as a "Hispanic-American," as someone outside the cultural center of the country. He wants to show instead that he is very much in the center of the culture; his book is the tale of how he lost his Hispanic-American past. With this understanding, the puzzling Shakespearean references in the opening sentences of the prologue begin to make sense. He is placing his book in the center of English-speaking culture, in the company of the central figure of English literature.

Rodriguez does not merely want his readers to see him as a Shakespearean scholar; he wants us to be puzzled about how a "socially disadvantaged" Hispanic-American comes to introduce his life via Shakespearean allusions. He himself is puzzled about how he has been so completely transformed. His introduction jumps from one kind of language to another and from scene to scene because his book is about how he has been jarred out of his childhood world. He wants to take his readers through some of his experience, to share the uncertainty and questioning that led him to write his book.

Rodriguez is so concerned about the mistaken assumptions his readers will have about him that he structures much of his prologue as a kind of debate. For example, in paragraphs 13–21, Rodriguez alternates between citing what other people have mistakenly said about him and correcting those people. In paragraphs 29 and 30 he similarly quotes what his editor wants him to do in his book, and goes on to explain why he will not follow that advice.

In paragraphs 26–28, Rodriguez defines his book as a "middle-class pastoral." Students may never have heard of a pastoral, so it might be useful to have them read the classic short poem "The Passionate Shepherd to His Love" by Christopher Marlowe. It celebrates the rural life but describes the shepherds as dressed in gold, coral, and amber. In other words, it is a rich person's view of what it is like to live a rural life. Rodriguez's point in paragraph 27 is that the pastoral is false praise; the rich people enjoy dreaming about being poor, about living a simpler life, but have no real desire to give up their wealth and power. Another way to bring students to understand the falseness of the pastoral is to have them think about how advertising uses scenes of happy country life to sell urban pleasures such as cigarettes, alcohol, and even jewels (look through any *New Yorker*).

Once students can see how someone can sing the praises of something he has no real desire for, they will understand better Rodriguez's ambivalent attitude toward his childhood. He praises that childhood for the intimacy it provided, an intimacy he has lost; but he believes what he has received in trade for that intimacy — public success — is worth more. He also believes that people must choose; they cannot have both the intimacy and public success. That is the conclusion that makes Rodriguez's book so disconcerting; all people want to believe that they can become well educated and successful without losing the kind of personalities and relationships they had before they sought to rise in the world.

Rodriguez drops much of the disconnected style of his prologue in the body of his book. But he keeps some of the uncertainty of his prologue alive in his first chapter. He switches back and forth between reminiscence and general discussion of bilingual education. The transitions are not as jarring as the leaps in the prologue, but they still surprise us: he keeps cutting off what he is doing and then taking it up again later, making us wait to make sense of it all. While he is creating new puzzles, Rodriguez also clears up some of the puzzles raised in the prologue. For example, in this chapter we can begin to understand the allusion to Caliban that began the prologue. We see how he has taken Caliban's advice, has "stolen their books" and "will have some run of this isle": he has gained power over some of the books that early in his life belonged only to *los gringos*. He does not clear up all the puzzles (why is he against affirmative action?); he leaves some questions to be answered in later chapters.

## Connections to Other Essays

For notes on essays about minority and immigrant experiences, see the instructor's manual entry on Maxine Hong Kingston, "The Woman Warrior."

In "Aria," Rodriguez creates a bittersweet reminiscence of his childhood that could be compared to the other reminiscences in this collection. For notes on essays about childhood, see the instructor's manual entry on Eudora Welty, "The Little Store."

## PAULA SISLER, "The Water Lily," page 496

### Teaching Strategies

Paula Sisler's essay exemplifies the fine composition students can produce when they use their own experience as a basis for writing. The assignment was to write a descriptive essay about a childhood event that must be recalled in concrete detail by "watching and observing adults."

The essay is deceptively simple. Using the boat, The Water Lily, as a focus for the multiple points she makes, Sisler describes not merely the obsessive interest her father has in the project but the relationships between friends, husband and wife, child and parents that are centered on the project. Students are often perplexed when they are asked to write from memory, noting that much of the detail seems to have escaped with time. Moreover, trying to re-create the feelings of a child may seem impossible, yet Sisler demonstrates the subconscious reservoir that memories occupy. We need to encourage students to understand the richness of memory, the complex impressions that are always there beneath the surface of events. The scents of autumn, the freshening of a lake breeze, the colors of a flower do not awaken in us single impressions but are tied to memories that intensify our understanding of moment. Writing about the multiplicities of our responses, what they remind us of, what other scenes flash in our minds — these are the clues that lead us as writers on that fascinating trail of re-creating experience.

"The Water Lily" is on one level a boat. But it is also a metaphor for the complicated experiences that Sisler recalls. We see the various characters and events through the focus of the boat. The friends, Arnie and Twilah, the wonderful glasses and shoes that depict Twilah's tacky outfits, the mother's patience and later rebellion, the episode of the near drowning all have heightened significance because the boat objectifies the emotional entanglement of their lives. Sisler enters into the re-created world with a sharp sense of how it felt and seemed. She is the child fearing to enter the water, trailing her hands in the iridescent waves, stuffing herself with sandwiches and strawberry soda. Her mastery of descriptive detail will provide students with a compelling example of how sensory detail helps readers to make emotional connections.

Students sometimes find themselves in a quandary: if they are to tell about a childhood memory, are they obliged to tell the "truth"? While Sisler may not recall exactly what happened, she knows the general truth of her experience and it is that reality which she brings forward with such dramatic vigor, making it seem as if the event had just happened. The "truth," then, is not a factual recitation of what happened — a kind of "first, then, next, and finally" sequence — but an interpretation of an event.

Students should also note the leisurely nature of the narrative. No detail is too small to escape Sisler's recollections, yet no detail appears excessive. The organization of the essay is structured by the metaphor of the boat, which allows the writer at the end to bring events forward to the final dissolution of the marriage, "the hull of the family drifting toward destruction." The end itself provides a surprise. While we may understand that the parents quarrel, given the childlike simplicity of the narrative we are not entirely prepared for the emotional toll that the "lovely water lily" has taken. Yet we are also satisfied, given the careful recapitulation, that the end was inevitable.

### Further Suggestions for Reading, Writing, and Discussion

A number of essays provide examples of descriptive writing used to elaborate emotional states. Some of the essays deal with observation, such as Beverly Dipo's "No Rainbows, No Roses" (page 115) and Dianne Emminger's "The Exhibition" (page 138); others exemplify the richness of recollections: Ann Louise Field's "The Sound of Angels" (page 147), David Landmann's "The House" (page 309), William G. Hill's "Returning Home" (page 138); Patrick Kinder Lewis's "Five Minutes North of Redding" (page 320), and An-Thu Quang Nguyen's "Tâi Con" (page 402).

Before assigning an essay that stresses descriptive detail, students might wish to read these essays and note the different ways in which the writers have used sensory impression as an organizing principle.

An-Thu Quang Nguyen's preface to "Tâi Con" describes a coloring game in which the child fills in the sensation or color first and then the outline or experience last. Students might try a memory exercise that begins with describing a sensation — feelings about a thunderstorm, for example — and then attempt to re-create a childhood experience of a storm.

**Instructor's Comments:** *David Borofka, Kings River Community College*

First, keep asking questions: the old journalistic stand-bys — who? what? when? where? why? how? — and those questions keep us in the concrete world of the senses — what does it look like? sound like? taste like? smell like? feel like? And keep asking those questions until we are no longer presenting a cliché or merely repeating an observation we've been taught; instead, we are truly re-creating, making experience anew, seeing that person, that place, that object for the first time.

Second, listen to yourself. I don't mean the old, bad advice of "Write the way you talk." I mean — listen to the "voices" of Orwell and Singer and Hughes and Sisler. In each we hear a signature, a fingerprint of written sound, a unique manner of expression that has as much to do with the structure of sentences and diction as it has to do with a way of seeing the world.

## JAMES JOYCE, "Araby," page 507

### Teaching Strategies

James Joyce's descriptions make almost everything in "Araby" radiate with symbolic meaning. But all Joyce does is *suggest* broad meanings; he does not specify them precisely. Encourage students to come up with their own interpretations; it would be hard to be "wrong." The tale can be taken as revealing the end of all romance or the beginning of the possibility of true love; as showing the triumph of religion over natural feelings or the end of religion's power; as the destruction of childhood purity and innocence or the rising out of cheap lust. Some of these might seem to fit better with the rest of Joyce's writings, but this short story is intriguingly ambiguous enough to support all of them — and even wilder interpretations. If you tell students that critics disagree about this story and do not let the class try to settle on any "right" interpretation, you can free discussion and stimulate the students' ingenuity.

All interpretations will have to take into account some basic elements of the tale — the religious language, the sexual innuendo, the stifling atmosphere in the community, and the mystifying and wonderful last line. But these elements can be put together in many different ways. To help students develop an overall interpretation, ask them why the narrator would still be thinking about these fairly insignificant events twenty or thirty years later, when he is writing this story. What is it about this relationship that never went anywhere that makes it a major event in the narrator's life?

To answer this question, students will have to decide on the symbolic meaning of the details in the tale. For example, the narrator's descriptions of Mangan's sister suggest that he views her as some sort of religious figure — he bears her "chalice"; his body becomes a "harp" playing in praise of her; she is the only thing described as lighted in this otherwise dark world. She could represent the glimmer of hope of some true religion in the narrator's debased world, or she could represent the end of religion, the worship of the false fire of lust. It all depends on whether we believe the narrator when he speaks of her as an ideal or whether we pay more attention to his watching the border of her petticoat.

The narrator goes to Araby to buy Mangan's sister a present; this could be his attempt to go on a crusade into the Orient to bring back tribute to his goddess. The bazaar could even represent escape from Ireland, an attempt to go East to another culture. Or the bazaar could stand for the turning of everything into commodities, the commercialization even of romance and religion.

Clearly the boy becomes disillusioned with his dreams of going to Araby and winning Mangan's sister's love, but whether this disillusionment is a bitter ending of all romance or the escape from false, cheap dreams to some kind of "true" life is left unclear. The religious language of the last line is so strong that readers could argue that the narrator finally has discovered true religious humility. On the other hand, the ending could represent the narrator's giving up all belief in anything, a cynical recognition that all is vanity. If we separate Joyce from the narrator, we might see the narrator as believing himself better for having escaped his cheap and false dreams, while Joyce regards the narrator as a sad person who has had all the romance and natural joy of life (including sexual joy) beaten out of him by a heartless society. The bazaar could represent the possibility of escape from Ireland by going East, an escape Joyce himself made, but an escape this narrator will fail to make because he will accept the Irish vision that all that is outside secure Catholic Ireland is sinful and tawdry.

The conversation the narrator overhears at the bazaar is a fine example of insignificant details that can carry great weight. The narrator hears an argument in which a girl claims she did not say something, and two English "gentlemen" say she did. This nonconversation, in which we never even know what the girl is accused of saying, has great meaning to the narrator. Some possible interpretations: (1) The conversation might make him aware that Mangan's sister has never said much of anything to him; he has thought about her a great deal, but all his interactions with her are imagined. The very emptiness of the conversation may represent to him the emptiness of his relationship with Mangan's sister. (2) This conversation might make him aware of how tawdry sexual flirtations can be. The Englishmen may be teasing the girl because she is Irish; this teasing may represent the rape of Ireland, the forcing of the poor Irish to toil for the more powerful and richer English. The narrator may see himself as joining in the worship of money and of "the Eastern kingdom" (England), which sets "eastern guards" on Ireland.

Some students might want to argue that this tale simply has no meaning; that Joyce is so ambiguous that he has failed to say anything. The class might discuss why Joyce would purposely want to make his story ambiguous. Some critics have argued that Joyce did not believe there is any single meaning to any event. The story could show that we are caught in language and institutions (religion, capitalism) that so determine our thoughts and actions that we cannot discover "truth" at all; all we have is what is offered by the communities we are raised in and, as alternatives, only socially provided illusions of escape (like the bazaar).

## Connections to Other Essays

This story pits a romantic idealization of life against a cynical, realistic view. Much of how individual readers interpret the story will depend on whether those readers believe that everyone needs some romantic illusions. E. B. White's reverie "Once More to the Lake" (page 39) also pits illusions against harsh reality and also leaves us uncertain which the author prefers.

James Joyce's story gives us a particularly complex and ambivalent view of childhood and its illusions. For some notes on other essays in this collection that touch on this topic, see the instructor's manual entry on Eudora Welty, "The Little Store."

## JOHN CLYDE THATCHER, "On Killing the Man," page 515

Thatcher's essay is a process analysis, a step-by-step explanation of how to trap small animals. However, Thatcher enlarges his analysis by depicting how it feels to be a hunter, drawing on experience to record feelings and insights. Accompanying the discussion is a steady stream of observations that evoke clear images of what it is like to be alone in a wintry wood: "My booted feet scarred the frosted grass. The traps slung over my shoulder tolled a death knell as they slapped against my back."

But there is an even larger purpose to the essay. It becomes apparent in paragraph 10 that Thatcher uses the trapping to underscore his transition to manhood, explaining that his decision to give up hunting is a recognition that the "boy must kill 'the man,' the one he has dreamed for himself." The last part of the essay expands into an impressive discussion of values, taking it beyond the more matter-of-fact explanations of trapping that appear in the opening paragraphs.

A point of class discussion might be the shift in narrative voice from the ironic, self-conscious tone at the beginning, where Thatcher seems to mock his ambition to grow up, to the more serious and purposeful comments that characterize the concluding portion. Thatcher appears to have finally discovered the purpose for his essay when he says, "I didn't kill him well because he was my first murder, and the hot tears that burst from me blinded my eyes." Question 4 in the main text addresses this problem, suggesting the need to clarify the narrative focus by deleting the earlier, gratuitous comments that undercut the seriousness of the point Thatcher finally achieves.

For a fuller discussion of Thatcher's essay see Part II, Chapter 4, "Responding to Professional Editing."

## Further Suggestions for Reading, Writing, and Discussion

Brad Manning's essay (page 369) is, in a sense, about "killing the man" — in his case his father — to grow up. A class discussion might center on what the two writers have learned from the rituals they engage in and the steps necessary to emerge from those rituals as adults. What is the cost for each? What is the lesson for all of us?

## Instructor's Comments: *Sylvia Vance, Otterbein College*

A primary strength of John Thatcher's essay is that it is solidly based on a personal experience of some real weight, effectively described and utilized to make an important point. The writing is compelling; the ending cannot be anticipated.

John showed me a rough draft of this essay, according to our usual procedures. I read it through, and — instead of making this suggestion or that, as I always do — I just said, "John, that's good."

## DORIS LESSING, "The Old Chief Mshlanga," page 522

### Teaching Strategies

Lessing's story offers an opportunity to discuss point of view and myths. The context of the story is set initially through the third-person point of view (paragraphs 1–4). It is not clear who the narrator is. Is it the girl grown up looking back at her life? Is it the impersonal voice of English society? Is this the omniscient voice of myth? The language often sounds like myths or fairy tales — "They were good, the years of ranging the bush." But there is also criticism of the girl — "This child could not see a msasa tree, or the thorn, for what they were."

Lessing's description evolves through comparison and contrast. In the rich setting of Africa, the child has created the imaginary world of a fairy-tale England.

The child, "whose eyes were sightless for anything but a pale willowed river, a pale gleaming castle," does not understand the beauty that surrounds her. It is the narrator who must provide the setting for the reader.

Contrast defines values as well. The child is "sightless" because that is how she has been taught to deal with her world. The attitudes of the white settlers are reflected in her responses to the natives she encounters. Even the language, "uncouth language which was by itself ridiculous," which she hears spoken daily, reinforces her inability to see and gives her a shared sense of superiority. She uses the Afrikaaners' terms to identify the various places in the bush.

There is also an implied contrast in the circumscribed white compound that sits inside the vast place of the Old Chief's country, a contrast the child notices later when she learns to see the difference between her father's farm, "a dirty and neglected place," and the Chief's village, where "the huts were lovingly decorated with patterns of yellow and red and ochre mud on the walls."

The story is about seeing Africa — not the mythic Africa the child has known where the natives and the land are viewed in terms of white needs, but the Africa of all its people, of ancient tribes and laws of property that are incomprehensible to the settlers. Even when the child attempts to question events, she is met "by an even greater arrogance of manner."

The shift in paragraph 14 to the first-person narrator, who has come forward frankly now to speak for her younger self, signals a shift in the way Africa will be perceived. The child becomes aware of the beauty around her, although her perception is still limited. The first encounter with the Old Chief reveals an emerging consciousness, which her subsequent reading begins to reinforce. Some attention should be paid to how Lessing structures the change and growth. Paragraphs 37–42 reveal the rhetorical patterns that reinforce the shift. Students might be asked to pick out the phrases that suggest change, for example: "As I read more books, I learned that the path . . . was the recognized highway for the migrants"; "Perhaps I even haunted it"; "Soon I carried a gun in a different spirit"; "And now the dogs learned better manners."

This is also the moment when the child begins to see the possibility of coexistence "to let both black and white people meet gently, with tolerance for each other's differences: it seemed quite easy." The discovery that the Chief's son works in the kitchen, however, reinforces the distance the young narrator must travel to bridge the two worlds, for it is the Chief's son who must take the mother's abuse while he bides his time. Later it is the son who is made to act as translator for his father in the scene where the fate of the goats is debated.

The child's journey to the Old Chief's village alters her understanding irrevocably. For the first time she discovers she is in an alien land. This is not the Africa of her father's home but a place that overwhelms, isolates, terrifies. Students should compare the descriptions of these passages (paragraphs 54–58) with the opening paragraphs, noting the differences in the kind of detail and the tone. Is it the child's imagination now unsettled by fear that makes her see danger everywhere just as earlier she saw castles and witches?

Students might also compare the places in the text where there is dialogue. The first time the child encounters the Old Chief, on a path near her farm, there is a courteous exchange, which is initiated by the Chief. He is the one who has undertaken a journey. It is this encounter that leads her to believe that black and white may coexist with mutual respect. The second time, it is the child who has undertaken the journey. The child must repeatedly ask to see the Chief. The dialogue reflects the distance between them. The exchange is stiff and unsatisfactory. The child thinks not of coexistence on the way home but of the hostility she has met, which is now reflected in the landscape: "I went slowly homewards, with an empty heart: I had learned that if one cannot call a country to heel like a dog, neither can one dismiss the past with a smile in an easy gush of feeling saying I could not help it. I am also a victim."

The concluding scene, the third example of dialogue involving the Old Chief, suggests how deep the hostility is and how unlikely any resolution. This time the Chief speaks through his son. There is no possibility of communication. The goats become the symbol of usurpation by the white farmers. The land the narrator's father has attempted to settle is the Chief's land. The narrator helps us to see how terrible the issues are by contrasting "this pathetic ugly scene, doing no one any good," with the beauty of the setting (paragraph 81). The story ends on an ambiguous note posing the resettlement, the sight of the abandoned village, the paradise that the settler has inherited, one against the other, offering little hope even for those like the narrator who have come to see.

The policeman speaks the final word for the white settlers, pointing out that the Chief's homestead, which has ancient claims on the land, "has no right to be there; it should have been moved long ago." But it is Africa the continent that truly has the last word. In a year, when the narrator seeks out the village again, the bush has taken over. And in the alley, where the plants grow, the next settler will "wonder what unsuspected vein of richness he had struck."

## Connections to Other Essays

Lessing is writing about realizing she is part of a minority that is hated by the majority in the land where she grows up. Her experience bears comparison to the other essays in this collection about the alienation of ethnic minorities (for notes on these essays, see the instructor's manual entry on "The Woman Warrior" by Maxine Hong Kingston). However, Lessing's experience differs from that of the other minority writers because she is part of a ruling minority, and the language she writes in is her minority's language, not the language of the majority. She is in a peculiar double position as both oppressor and oppressed; students might discuss which role she feels more strongly — in other words, does she feel guilt or anger about the injustice in Africa? The narrator in the story becomes uncomfortable with her role as a part of a ruling class but cannot easily change things. Being a child and a female, the narrator is oppressed herself. A central theme in this work is the problem of how an individual overcomes personal powerlessness to alter an unjust society.

**TODD UNRUH,** "No Respecter of Persons," page 535

### Teaching Strategies

Todd Unruh had a specific purpose in mind when he wrote this essay. "My intent was to slow the reader down in thinking of his life and pursuits and learn to respect others' lives more. I wanted the reader to have a new feeling about the significance of life."

The essay is organized around a series of contrasts. There are the comparisons between what Unruh calls the "frivolity around death and funerals, such as the expensive caskets and vault and flowers," and the sobering nature of his task. There are the contrasts between the writer and his more experienced and more jaded fellow workers. There are the contrasts between the death of the old man and that of the young child. One of the strengths of the essay is the reflective nature of Unruh's observations. Like Brad Manning, who recounts his adolescent struggles with his father (page 369), Unruh wants the reader to see beyond the literal experience to the philosophical questions that trouble him.

The sharpness of the detail in this essay derives from his discomfort. He cannot ignore sensory impressions — the smell of the moldy earth, the heaviness of the casket, the dirty window through which he views the proceedings — yet he does not linger over detail for its own sake. The narrative is terse: dialogue is used to underscore the matter-of-fact nature of his co-workers. Even his reflections are blunt: "I wondered if our grave crew, like society, hadn't treated the old man's death just as those around him had treated the old man's last few years."

The experience forces Unruh to question his values much the way that Beverly Dipo's description (page 115) of a dying woman forces her to wonder at the way we treat people. Both confront death on a number of levels and try to integrate the ordinariness of what they must do with the emotional debt they must pay.

Unruh does not linger over the experience, recognizing that his point can be made economically. Students might note the restraint with which he describes what he does and the reflective questions that extend his point. The essay is a good example of purpose determining length. Too often, students are concerned with issues of length, as if the number of pages in and of itself proved the seriousness of the subject. In Unruh's case the writer accomplishes his intent to "slow the reader down" with a brief but telling narrative.

### Further Suggestions for Reading, Writing, and Discussion

Several student essays deal with the confrontation of dying and death. While it may be the kind of subject that makes students feel uncomfortable, nevertheless, the pervasiveness of the theme in these essays suggests that students will often create an opportunity to explore their feelings in writing. See the essays by Celeste Barrus (page 47) and Beverly Dipo (page 115) in this edition, as well as those of Max Ramsey and Frances E. Taylor in the second edition of *Student Writers at Work*, and Joanne Menter in the first edition.

### Instructor's Comments: *Don McDermott, Oklahoma State University*

I think the best advice I can give to students writing about their experience is to re-create in their minds before they even begin to write a dramatic visualization of the event.

I like to read a lot of student papers to the students who write them. Very quickly the students realize that they are writing to a larger audience, and students give better feedback to the writers when they feel that their ideas are being considered not just by the writer but by the entire group (including the instructor, for whom they always want to appear interested and involved).

### PHYLLIS ROSE, "Tools of Torture: An Essay on Beauty and Pain," page 543

### Teaching Strategies

This essay demonstrates how a writer can transform her own experience, leading herself and her readers to odd and delightful conclusions. In the first part of the essay, Rose transforms our sense of implements of torture, making us admire their ingenuity. She writes with such relish and what she is describing is so grotesque that she makes us laugh at torture, undercutting our usually pious and moral reaction. Her comparison of torture and French cuisine is unexpected but plausible because she has described the details of pain with such exuberance as to render them delicious.

Rose uses white space to switch to another scene and another subject — facials, beauty treatments. By using white space and not stating a transition, she makes us think about parallels between visiting the torture museum and visiting the beauty parlor. The parallels make us smile. We might guess that she is going to criticize beauty treatments as self-inflicted torture, forced on women by sexist society (like foot-binding). But she does not move to that conclusion at all. Instead, she describes beauty treatments and torture as sharing a similar "aesthetic"; both involve a "rich diversity" of bodily treatments. The first five paragraphs present unusual views, but in paragraph 6 Rose twists our thinking even further. Her essay changes rather drastically as she moves away from creating scenes and begins abstract analysis. To make sense of torture, she takes us through several intellectual contexts — history, psychological theory, and Judith Shklar's book (which most people probably have not heard of and do not need to know to understand this essay).

Finally, she brings these intellectual ideas and her personal experience together to draw, in the last two paragraphs, the most startling conclusions of her essay. She argues that fashion, beauty treatments, and the pursuit of frivolity may provide the best antidotes to torture. Since earlier in the essay she seemed to be equating beauty treatments and torture, this conclusion is surprising. Moreover, she seems to invert everything we have been taught about morality when she says that "selfish frivolity" is the "moral touchstone" our age needs. Moral people are supposed to be unselfish and serious, aren't they? It is hard to imagine the value of taking a frivolous attitude toward racism, pollution, or nuclear war.

The style of the last paragraph also seems to undercut her argument. Phrases like "moral touchstone" and "radical hedonism" seem too serious for an essay arguing that one should not take one's goals too seriously. But we can see that Rose is quite frivolous in this essay — in the beginning. Her initial descriptions show us how to treat torture frivolously, to laugh at it, to see it as "merely kinky." She shows how hedonism overwhelms moral fervor, leaving us laughing and delighted instead of solemnly indignant. Torture is so horrifying that if we take it seriously we are likely to justify the killing (or torturing) of people who torture. She wants us instead to laugh. Such a change in tone in our approach to moral issues is precisely what she is arguing for.

The two halves of Rose's essay illustrate the freedom essay writers have. In the first part, she entertains and enlightens merely by describing something in detail but with the "wrong" tone. She shows how merely describing something can lead to discoveries if we do not settle for the obvious and already known views. In the second part, she shows how freely a writer can move among intellectual ideas. Paying attention to fleeting, odd thoughts might lead students to similarly surprising conclusions.

## Connections to Other Essays

"The Blanket Party" by Terry L. Burns (page 76) suggests that torture is a regular part of military discipline. His analysis is similar to Rose's; he shows that ordinary people will become torturers when they become a "faceless" part of a group or institution. A selfish frivolity would probably prevent people from believing in the rigid military way of life.

"The Use of Force" by William Carlos Williams (page 57) shows a doctor turning to violence and in a sense torturing a patient. Williams, like Rose, shows how good intentions pursued too far and with too much intensity can lead to the inflicting of pain on others.

**TOR VALENZA,** "At Diane's," page 549

## Teaching Strategies

Valenza's assignment was to write a personal essay on any topic. Valenza chose to write a eulogy. Diane's still exists, but it is the changes that have taken place in the author's life that are the subject of the tribute.

The essay has a clear pattern organized around stages in his life. Valenza sets the stage in the opening paragraph, introducing the place — Diane's; the street — Columbus Avenue; the time — prior to Ed Koch's election to mayor; the friends — Alisa, Brian, Tanya — without lingering over explanations. The developing chronology is marked by changes that occur in each of the categories. Students should note how economically the setting and the friendship are described. The changing price of hamburgers helps to focus the shifts in time; the conversations of the friends mark their growing maturity. Each paragraph offers a bit more insight into the complexity of their relationship; our understanding becomes a cumulative one. Students are often baffled by description, especially when it pertains to friendship. How much should be explained? What kind of physical detail should be included? Valenza has found a means to describe friends without telling us directly what they looked like. We "see" them through conversation, interests, and actions, and we feel we "know" them by the repetition of their concerns as they enter each new stage.

The last paragraph acts as a recitative of the themes established at the beginning of the essay. It also serves to remind us that the coming changes will undoubtedly obliterate not only a place but childhood.

## Further Suggestions for Reading, Writing, and Discussion

Valenza's essay is deceptively simple. It should offer students an excellent opportunity to examine some phase in their own lives in which they mark the successive stages in terms of places, people, actions, and setting. Students might also examine the multiple applications of the chronological structure.

## Instructor's Comments: *John Elder, Middlebury College*

This course uses computers as the vehicle for exchange of writing. All of the students' entries and exchanges are done on microcomputers and transferred to the college's mainframe. Each week students in the course respond to the entries of two colleagues. On the basis of this "correspondence," further work in small groups and with the class as a whole on drafting, revising, and editing sustains an energetic and constructive quality. Students know and care about each other as writers and as persons.

Word processing has been a wonderful help to me in encouraging students to see writing as an adventurous process carried out within a community.

## JO GOODWIN PARKER, "What Is Poverty?" page 555

## Teaching Strategies

Parker's essay is structured very subtly by the repetitions within it. In the first paragraph, the repetition of the word "Listen" creates the relationship of the speaker to "you," the reader. We are not pleasantly drawn into this essay; we are commanded to pay attention. The repeated command is slightly irritating because it suggests that we are not willing to obey — and throughout the essay the speaker reacts as if "you," the readers, are a hostile audience. We are being directly attacked by this essay. At the end, the speaker explains that she has been trying to make us angry so that we will react. This essay does not end with a conclusion, but with a return to the spirit of the opening, a question that feels like a command addressed to us, demanding that we speak up.

Throughout the essay, the word "you" recurs, used in at least two different ways. Sometimes it seems to address a specific person who is responding to Parker's arguments (paragraphs 4 and 12). Sometimes it is a general "you" that the narrator uses to describe her own situation in general terms — what "you" do when you are poor. Both uses of "you" make readers uncomfortable — either we are unsympathetic creeps or we are terribly poor. Further, by blurring the distinction between the two senses of "you," Parker refuses to let readers separate themselves from the poor.

The uncomfortableness of the relationship of speaker to readers is increased by all the repetitions in the essay. It would be bad enough to have to hear about all the suffering of the poor, but to have to hear about it over and over again makes us feel claustrophobic, stuck in a small room with a person repeatedly telling us painful stories. There is no escape from the voice in this essay, as there is no escape from poverty.

Even with all the repetitions, Parker creates a sense of movement through an argument. She starts with the physical properties of poverty (smell, tiredness, dirt), then shifts to emotional, mental effects (asking for help, being embarrassed, remembering), turns to long-term, institutional issues (schools, health care), and ends with dreams of the future. The ending hints at a small possibility of escaping the endless cycle of poverty. The narrator says, "I have come out of my despair to tell you this." Her despair is not complete; she has a small hope that her audience will do something.

The hope underlying this essay might, however, merely be evidence that the person writing this essay is not actually living the poverty she describes. This might be an essay written by a person who is fairly well-off, someone who does not know what it is like to have no hope at all. We have to ask ourselves finally whether this entire essay is a fraud. Students might discuss what features make this essay believable and what features might suggest that Parker is not speaking from personal experience.

### Connections to Other Essays

Parker's essay addresses an imaginary audience as "you" and so could fit into the unit on second-person point of view, the unit based on Earnestine Johnson's "Thank you Miss Alice Walker" (page 259).

Ann Louise Field in "The Sound of Angels" (page 147) also discusses the effects of poverty on a family. David Landmann in "The House" (page 309) addresses the issue of the invisibility of the poor. Like Parker, he challenges middle-class readers to listen to the voice of a poor person.

# PART II

## STUDENT WRITERS AT WORK

### Chapter 1
### Revising Drafts

Throughout the book we have offered students polished prize-winning essays to study. In this chapter, we offer students the chance to see how three such essays were composed. Too often students think that first drafts resemble final drafts and imagine that fluent writing must have flowed just as smoothly from the writer's pen. These misconceptions students hold about the composing process often sabotage their best efforts. This chapter aims to show students the scratch-outs and the drafts, the decisions and conversations that occurred in the writers' minds to produce their essays. Students can see how ideas begin, grow, and become good writing.

This chapter begins with a detailed examination of the process by which Barbara Seidel wrote her essay "A Tribute to My Father." We then present the drafts Brad Manning wrote for his essay "Arm-Wrestling with My Father." It is probably most effective to have students go back to where Manning's essay first appears in the book (pages 369–374) and then to work with the students through the successive drafts that led to his prize-winning essay.

## Getting Started

Students should be encouraged to discuss Seidel's method of getting started — brainstorming. Many students are unfamiliar with this method of thinking as quickly and as broadly as possible about a subject by writing down everything that springs to mind. Seidel's brainstorming sheets are interesting because they are rich with information. She brainstormed a generous supply of details that, as she reports, "served as a road map, pointing me where I should focus my attention and helping me to see how I wanted to view my subject."

It is helpful for students to brainstorm together on a common topic so they can see how the method works. For such an exercise, the teacher offers a topic and writes all responses on the blackboard for the whole class to see. Students are always intrigued by how easily and quickly they can brainstorm so much information.

After brainstorming together for ten to fifteen minutes, students should move on to the next step, finding a focus. As they look at all the information they have brainstormed, ask them to consider what details seem most interesting, what details could be developed, and how the details could be grouped to provide a focus.

## Drafting

Seidel's first draft provides for a good discussion on many aspects of composing. First, she used her notes, but she went beyond these when she found that she needed new information. Fresh ideas came out in the writing process, and Seidel was open and receptive, following her writing where it took her. As she reports: "I just let loose in writing this first draft so that I could connect all my notes and the ideas that were still rushing through my head. If I try to be too orderly in the first draft then I am stymied. A first draft is always an experiment: I am still testing and exploring what I want to write." Too often students become slaves to the notes, outlines, or thesis statements they develop prior to writing their first drafts. Beginning writers should realize that new possibilities will emerge as they learn from their first drafts what they want to write. As James Joyce commented, "It is in the writing that the good things come out."

Second, Seidel did not bother to edit her draft or worry about mistakes she might have made in it. Students can learn from Seidel that there is plenty of time for editing later after a writer has figured out what he or she wants to write. Writers need to have different standards of judgment for their first and final drafts.

## Revising

Students should be asked to define their revising practices and to compare their methods with those of Seidel. From research on the composing processes of college freshmen, we know that most students do not see revision as the larger process of questioning the meaning of their essays. Rather, they assume that once they have written a first draft the meaning is established and they need only change words and correct mistakes. Thus, most students think of revising as a superficial reviewing of a fixed draft. Instead of reading their drafts in order to re-envision the meaning of the text, most students merely proofread their drafts.

Seidel, however, is a student writer who has learned about the value of taking time and patience to revise. As she reports: "Most of my time 'writing' is really revising. . . . It is only through revising that I can keep refining my writing and hope to reach my readers." We see Seidel at work in this section, thinking about her ideas and questioning her purpose.

Seidel's major concern as she revised was that she had not captured her father's personality and achieved her purpose in writing about him. She realized that she had interjected too many of her opinions and that she had to remove herself from the essay. As she tells us: "I wanted my father to tell his own story. I wanted to show that his actions speak louder than his words. I shortened my sentences to let simple statements and his actions speak for themselves."

Seidel's final draft is presented alongside her first draft so that students can study her major decisions and changes. Students will be able to see that revision is a re-envisioning of the *whole* text.

Decisions cannot be made in isolation; they must support each other so that the writing moves forward smoothly and logically. If decisions are inconsistent, they will work against each other and result in awkward and confused writing. Revision cannot be piecemeal; it must be governed by a writer's controlling purpose.

As an exercise in revision, students should study their own drafts and classify the types of changes they have made. Ask them to offer explanations for their changes. The point of this exercise is to help students determine whether any pattern or guide controls their revising process, or if their changes are made without a concern for the whole text.

**Exercise: Three Drafts by Brad Manning**

We have provided several drafts of Brad Manning's essay "Arm-Wrestling with My Father" to help students understand and appreciate the decisions and changes Manning made as he wrote and revised his essay. There are appreciable differences between Manning's drafts, and students should have little difficulty recognizing these differences. Questions are included after each draft so that students can better evaluate not only the strengths and weaknesses of each draft but also the process by which Manning achieved his purpose in revising.

One useful exercise is to have students summarize what Manning achieved in revising. We aim in this chapter to help students to understand that revision is a process of questioning, deciding, and changing — a process that occurs *throughout* the composing process. Manning's drafts offer students an excellent opportunity to see a writer at work making the changes that strengthen the meaning and purpose of writing an essay.

## Chapter 2

## Peer Editing

The purpose of this chapter is to encourage and help train student writers to respond effectively to one another's essays. The chapter opens with detailed advice to peer editors on how to respond to another student's essay. A demonstration of the techniques of peer editing follows, as four composition students read and react to Patrick Kinder Lewis's prize-winning essay "Five Minutes North of Redding." This section is followed by detailed advice to writers on how to work most productively with the comments of peer editors. Then Patrick Lewis reads the responses of four peer editors, revises his essay in light of what they have to say, and explains why he accepted many of their comments and rejected others. Students are invited to practice peer editing both with another student's prize-winning essay, Johnna Lynn Benson's "Rotten at the Core," and with their own essays. There are numerous ways to use peer editing, and the process we describe here is not definitive. Whatever procedure you decide to use, this section illustrates for students some of the many ways they can respond to one another's papers.

If you have had your students work successfully in small groups on one another's essays, you will need little encouragement to see the benefits of peer editing. If the process is new to you, however, some consideration of the pedagogical value of peer editing may be in order. And let there be no misunderstanding: peer editing does not reduce the number of student essays an instructor will read. If anything, the peer editing process, given its encouragement of multiple drafts, may well increase the total number of essays an instructor responds to each semester. The principal benefit of peer editing is that instructors are far less likely to read many rough drafts (literally and figuratively). Each students whose essays have been peer edited will have prepared at least two full drafts of an essay before it is submitted to an instructor for an additional reading and a grade. In effect, the amount of time each of us spends responding to student writing may not decrease, but surely the quality of the papers we read will increase. Our experience suggests that essays that have been peer edited suffer from far fewer errors in mechanics, spelling, and grammar and, at the same time, show an increase in the writers' control of syntax, diction, and organization. But, perhaps most important, students who participate in peer editing come to appreciate that they are indeed writing for an audience beyond their instructors. Students will have *frequent* opportunities to hear their own voices as writers — some perhaps for the first time. Besides an immediate and enduring sense of audience, peer editing provides writers with a range of observations on and evaluations of their writing that will help them revise their work. The process also provides the peer editors with practice in reading and in writing since they must write suggestions about how their peers might improve their essays. In effect, the activities of peer editing enhance virtually every aspect of the writing and reading process.

"Peer Editing" reveals the complex interrelationship between writer and reader. However, it is important to point out that the exchange in this part took place between a writer — Patrick Lewis — and a group of readers at the Queens College in the City University of New York who had never met one another and who may have felt less threatened by the process because of the distance between them. This is not always the case in the classroom setting where writers and readers confront one another directly. If students, and instructors as well, have never had any experience with collaborative learning, the practice may seem unsettling at first. Moreover, there is a tendency to abandon group work at an early point if instructors do not make a philosophical commitment to the concept. To facilitate that commitment, it is necessary to look briefly at the conventional wisdom that collaborative learning refutes.

Collaborative learning is at odds with most educational practice. With the exception of the group activities that characterize the earliest years of schooling, the traditional classroom emphasizes the solitary nature of learning whereby students become increasingly more passive, increasingly more distant from the notion of learning for its own sake. Collaborative learning, on the other hand, stresses an active role for students and underscores the need for sharing and cooperation. It promotes learning as a means to generate and not merely consume ideas.

There may be considerable resistance to the concept of peer editing, and it can come from diverse quarters. Students who are unfamiliar with the principles of peer editing are often intimidated by the advice they receive from peers. Other students may be reluctant to comment on another student's work for fear of offending. But perhaps most often, it is the role of the instructor in the peer editing process that some students — and teachers — find disconcerting.

The idea of the instructor as *the* expert is deeply entrenched in our educational system. Traditionally, students are trained to work independently and often competitively and are expected to seek approval from and to accept the judgment of a single authority. Writing to please an instructor is a staple of student lore. In such circumstances, students usually write to avoid error rather than to express a clear sense of their thinking on a particular subject. But writing for an audience of peers upsets these traditional values and seems — on the surface — to undermine the role the teacher plays.

Peer editing in small groups realigns the politics of the classroom. The instructor becomes a partner in, not the primary instrument of, learning. As a result, some objections to peer editing arise from colleagues who are less than willing to relinquish a share of the control over a class. But the peer editing process doesn't reduce the role or the importance of the instructor. Rather it emphasizes that the responsibility and the authority for writing reside with the writer and not the teacher. Our leading researchers, theorists, and practitioners repeatedly argue that learning does not originate with the instructor but with the learner, that when students and instructors alike begin to work collaboratively the conditions for learning are improved considerably, the mode of learning is enriched, and the process is more deeply internalized. Like T. S. Eliot's magi, teachers who work daily in and with small groups are "no longer at ease . . . in the old dispensation."

The suggestions that follow are not a formula for success. They are the result of our trials and errors, of responses to the needs of our students as well as to our own needs as teachers. Working out a process that is successful will be as important to the development of small-group work as the fact of group work itself. If there are instructors at your institution who work with small groups, seek their advice. If you are setting out on the journey alone, find a few colleagues who are willing to undertake the project with you. Support and consultation will aid in helping you over the rough spots. Additional suggestions for group work are offered in the text.

The peer editing process usually involves two distinct phases with many different activities in each:

### The Peer Editor's Response to Writing:

The peer editor *listens to* and *reads* the draft of another student's essay.

The peer editor *works at understanding — and appreciating —* what the writer is trying to accomplish in this essay.

The peer editor *makes specific and nonjudgmental observations* about the essay.

The peer editor *summarizes* the main point of the essay and notes how the writer develops it in each paragraph.

The peer editor *writes* abundant comments about the draft, assessing both its general strengths and weaknesses and offering specific praise for what it has accomplished and suggestions about how it might be improved.

The peer editor *reads, discusses, clarifies, and amplifies* the written responses to the draft in conversation with the author.

The peer editor *helps the writer realize and articulate fully* the specific purpose and goals of the essay.

### The Writer's Response to Peer Editing:

The writer *reads* the peer editors' written responses to the draft.

The writer *seeks clarification and development* of responses that are unclear.

The writer *explains* such matters as the purpose of the draft, its intended audience, its main idea, and its supporting examples in conversation with the peer editors.

The writer *leaves the conversation with detailed written responses* to the draft that have been clarified and amplified in the discussion with the peer editors.

The writer *evaluates the responses* of the peer editors, *creates a list of priorities* from among them, and *develops a plan for revision* based on them.

The writer *prepares a new, more effective draft of the essay.*

The exact sequence and duration of the activities within each phase of the peer editing process depend on the writer's needs, the peer editors' collective experience in reading and writing, and the class's overall instructional goals and schedule. The specific procedures peer editors follow and the pace at which they work within each phase can also vary greatly. Yet, regardless of its length and place within the sequence, each phase of the peer editing process is designed to feature reading and writing as the primary and central activities in learning how to write more effectively.

Peer editors can work with other student writers one on one, in small groups, or within the class as a whole to help one another get started, write, revise, and edit their essays. Most often the process is applied to students working in small groups. Most teachers prefer to break their classes up into groups of four or five — especially if the class session runs for seventy-five minutes or longer. If less time is available, then a smaller group may be more appropriate. The size of the peer editing groups can be determined by whether each peer editor will have time to respond fully to the essay and whether each writer will have time to press the peer editor to clarify the points that need clarification.

Determining the make-up of each group may be wholly arbitrary (say, every fifth name on your class roster forms the first group, and so on) or planned (placing students whose native language is not English throughout the groups so that they benefit from practicing English with students who are more proficient). Late students can be added to the groups. Usually, there are five to six small roups in each writing class. The groups may be reorganized to meet instructional needs (such as grouping students with related compositional problems) or to reinvigorate the energy level of particular groups.

Students are asked to sit with their groups as soon as they come to class so that time is not lost rearranging the room and colleagues in other classrooms are not assaulted by the sound of chairs scraping across the floor. As the semester progresses, the noise level of the groups will rise, but it is the productive noise of writers and readers engaged in an absorbing enterprise. The instructor's voice is heard less as he or she comes to serve more as a resource person available whenever needed by an individual or a group.

The success of the groups may well depend on the specificity of the instructor's directions. The more specific your assignments, the more successful the exercise is likely to be. In "Peer Editing," we recommend that students begin the peer editing process by offering a description of what the writer has written in the form of nonjudgmental observations on the essay they have read or heard. Doing so gives the writer a clear and neutral sense of what he or she has written. For the purposes of peer editing, we define an *observation* as a statement about which there can be no disagreement. Yet many students have a good deal of difficulty maintaining the nonjudgmental response on which observations depend. Quite often, students rush to offer their *opinions* on what the writer has said. By restricting themselves — at least initially — to observations, students leave the authority for revision where it belongs, with the writer. To help students distinguish between observation and opinion, we sometimes recommend that they begin each of their statements with "I notice that," at least until sufficient practice making nonjudgmental observations no longer requires this prefatory phrase.

In addition to describing what they have read or heard, the peer editors are also expected to evaluate other students' writing. In "Peer Editing" we have outlined these distinct kinds of evaluative comments by peer editors:

1. Detailed marginal notations on the specific strengths and weaknesses of an essay.
2. A succinct summary of the main idea of the essay and an assessment of how fully the writer develops that controlling idea in each paragraph.
3. A general evaluative comment at the end of the essay, offering an overview of the essay's overall strengths and weaknesses and detailed recommendations and priorities for revising.

The example of the four composition students' response to Patrick Lewis's essay offers a wealth of teaching opportunities. In their detailed reactions, we can discover clear differences in what each looks for as a peer editor. Nicholas Balamaci, for example, spends a great deal of time discussing the diction and phrasing of Lewis's essay and seems to reserve his most extensive — and most persuasive — points for his summary comments at the end. In contrast, Jason Eskenazi seems more at ease — and more richly informative — in his specific marginal notations.

The peer editors' observations and evaluations may be made either directly on the photocopies (or mimeographed copies) of the manuscript the writer supplies to each peer editor or on a separate sheet of paper if the writer has read the essay aloud. In either event, the writer leaves each peer editing session with several responses to what he or she has written.

The process of peer editing depends on each student's being present and prepared to work collaboratively. Having a draft ready on the date assigned is a prerequisite for successful peer editing. Instructors needn't spend a great deal of time reminding students of this fact. Students who *are* prepared quickly take a dim view of those who aren't or who try to slide by with incomplete or shoddy work.

Initially, instructors might want to spend some time helping students feel at ease with each other in small groups. They might, for example, have students interview each other the first day, then write up the interview and present it to the group or the class. Or instructors might give students a "whodunit" problem to solve as a group and ask them to write their findings collectively and present them to the class. Or instructors might also assign each group a picture and ask them collectively to write a story about it.

Instructors might occasionally hear some students remark that they are enjoying themselves but that they wonder if they will actually learn anything from peer editing. We can honestly remind students that collaborative learning is indeed fun and getting to know one another is an important dimension of working collectively on improving one another's writing. In many commuter colleges, for example, most students have little extended contact with their peers except in their classes, and even there many remain isolated. Working collaboratively as writers and peer editors in small groups combats much of the isolation and passivity of the learning process.

Another potential problem to anticipate early in the peer editing process is that some students may at first be frightened to hear their words read aloud in the small groups. Talking directly and honestly about how each writer feels about presenting his or her essay in this context will help ease that initial anxiety and relax those hands that shook or those voices that trembled.

Most instructors find it productive to move around and listen during the peer editing sessions, counseling themselves to remember that their role is to help the writer and peer editors hear one another. Some instructors choose to write along with their students and share drafts of their own essays as a fully participating member of a small group. Still other instructors prefer to restrict themselves to the role of observer. Some keep a log of their observations and discuss what they have noticed with each of the small groups. In this respect, students are always surprised by how much there is to observe and are delighted by the fact that they are the source of so much productive interest. In most cases, the instructor comes rather quickly to be regarded as an especially resourceful voice that can help direct the peer editors' energy and clarify — and perhaps resolve — the particularly knotty compositional problems that invariably surface in each small group. Such a role is far removed from the traditional authoritarian image of the teacher lecturing about grammar in front of the class, and such a role may well inspire a good deal of good-spirited bantering.

But there may well be other times when the peer editing groups do not work so well. It undoubtedly will be especially useful to elicit the students' responses to the progress of their small groups as the semester proceeds. When a group reports that it is encountering difficulty, the instructor can spend a good deal more time working with that group while the other groups continue to advance. Generally, the "problem" is a simple matter of someone's shyness or reluctance to take control. At other times, one or more students need the instructor's additional encouragement. If you think it might help, try taping a peer editing session or two and let the peer editors and writers hear themselves. Who is doing most of the talking? Who is silent? What does each peer editor seem to focus on? But mostly, like good coaches, we ought to remind our students that we are committed to the processes of collaborative learning and peer editing, that we respect the kind of learning that is taking place, and that despite the mess and awkwardness of seemingly random comments, we recognize that students are becoming better writers and that they have developed a stronger voice and a surer sense of audience.

Frequently, students pause in the group's work and chat about other aspects of their studies or life. It is understandable that instructors might at first be especially concerned about what apparently is a waste of time. but if instructors were to keep a log, they would invariably note that the conversation always seems to come back to the essay, that the digressions are a way of making connections with the experience at hand, and that quite naturally, the writer has evoked memories that need to be shared. James Britton in *Language, the Learner, and the School* suggests that we have overlooked the complex richness of chatter as a way to

106

enhance the writing process. We might well be able to come to see such moments as valuable forays into the world of friendship and confine our nervousness to our logs.

We present in this manual and in the text itself a number of suggestions for encouraging the peer editing process. Let us close with a few final suggestions:

1. All observations and evaluations are most helpful when they are made in writing. Writing is the natural extension of thinking. It makes thinking recoverable. In the peer editing process, readers benefit from abundant exercises in putting their reactions in writing, and writers leave each peer editing session grateful and ready to read and act on the detailed written responses of their peers.

2. All writing should be read aloud. When students read aloud both their own essays and their responses to someone else's work, they not only will gain a much more vibrant sense of themselves as writers but will also be able to *hear* as well as *see* the particular strengths and weaknesses of their own work. They will come to appreciate better their responsibility for what they write — the essay or the peer editing comments are so demonstrably their own — and their authority over their writing. By listening, reading, and speaking carefully, students will invariably also become sensitive to writing as social transaction. Reading aloud and listening carefully are, after all, public, social, and even at times communal activities.

3. All decisions should be left to the writer. The peer editors help these decisions, but the authority and the responsibility for writing remain the writer's.

By working frequently and productively as peer editors on other students' writing, students can more readily relax into treating their own essays as works-in-progress. They can also build on their understanding of their specific strengths and weaknesses as writers and more confidently prepare better-crafted and more articulate final drafts. Eventually, they may well come to treat their own writing and that of their peers with the same dignity and generous critical attention that they have previously reserved for recognized works of literature. The goal, then, of peer editing — like that of the composing process itself — carries far beyond the classroom walls. Peer editing helps train students to explore and express fully the ideas, interests, and the experiences they value.

In addition, peer editing provides the writer with a permanent record of responses. Allowing students to test early drafts without penalty encourages them to take risks, to test ideas, to discover the needs of an audience, to uncover the writer in themselves. Perhaps of all the activities we undertake in college, teaching students to work effectively in a group best prepares them for the collaborative enterprises of the world at large. Group work teaches students kindness, patience, and self-respect. It teaches instructors to be listeners and observers. Everyone benefits.

## Chapter 3

## Moving from Personal Experience to
## Exposition and Argument

The principles we encourage students to understand and practice in this chapter are central to the overall purpose of *Student Writers at Work and in the company of other writers.* We aim to help students recognize and develop their own skills as writers, as resourceful people able to express a clear sense of the ideas they value with practiced confidence. To exercise increasing authority over their own ideas, student writers need to appreciate fully the intellectual connections between one part of their essay and another, between one idea and another, and between one course and another. To help make such connections habitual, we have focused this chapter on how students can recognize and develop their own resourcefulness as writers by discovering in personal-experience essays ample resources for writing expository and argumentative ones.

Moving from personal experience to exposition and argument need not be haphazard. We outline a series of steps on page 680 that students can follow as they seek to move beyond personal experience. Asking students to reread their personal-experience essays aloud several times should provide practiced readers with several new subjects to explore in expository or argumentative essays. For less-practiced readers, we describe fundamental intellectual "moves" to help them recognize ample subjects for expository and argumentative essays. For each of these moves — from specific to general, from autobiography to biography, from concrete to abstract, and from observation to inference — we provide a series of questions designed to assist student writers in recognizing and developing the connections between one subject and another. We try throughout this chapter to make explicit what is implicit in each of these moves: broadening the point of view, the purpose, and the audience addressed. To expand one's vision beyond autobiography is to practice mastery of a skill that enables one to participate with energy and authority in the spirited conversations (in discussions and in writing) of the intellectual community.

Instructors can help students discover new subjects for expository and argumentative papers by encouraging them to identify the issues embedded in their essays and then to broaden their point of view on these issues. Any of the exercises you use to develop your students' control of point of view would work well here to help them discover the distance (first to third person) and breadth of vision (self to others) necessary to explore a subject to explain it or argue convincingly about it.

Generating ideas about a subject might at first prove especially difficult for some students. Yet turning to such proven "idea-generators" as brainstorming and freewriting should help ease students into their own eloquence — and rather quickly. Working in small groups, both in conversation and in writing, also helps students to generate as many ideas about a subject as possible.

Deciding on a new subject to write about — as Beverly Dipo and Curtis Chang so clearly report in this chapter — is the difficult part of moving from personal

108

experience to exposition and argument. Encourage students to trust their instincts and intelligence: Which subjects are they most interested in writing about? Which are they most interested in learning most about?

Many students do not understand the difference between having an idea about a subject and asserting an idea about a subject. In the former, the idea remains loosely stated, with no clear sense of direction or purpose. In the latter, the idea is presented in specific terms, which control the contents and course of each sentence in the essay.

The sample essays written by Beverly Dipo and Curtis Chang highlight the frustrations and the satisfactions of each of the recommended steps in developing expository and argumentative essays out of personal experience. The processes that Dipo and Chang engage in illustrate how writers can be increasingly self-sufficient as they work with the standard forms of academic discourse. Mastering the skill of moving from personal experience to exposition and argument will overcome a frustration most students share, however unwittingly, with their instructors — that is, that the essays they write don't seem to be connected in any productive way. By recognizing and exploring the connections between one idea and another and between one essay and another, student writers can appreciate more readily the common threads that weave together the seemingly disparate verbal elements of their lives.

# Chapter 4
## Responding to Professional Editing

In this final chapter of the book, we give students the opportunity to see a professional editor at work, offering suggestions for revision and shaping the essays as if for publication in a magazine. We have included this chapter because observing a professional editor at work can teach students important lessons about the role of revision in the composing process.

We invited Jane Aaron, a professional editor, to edit John Clyde Thatcher's essay. Aaron edited the essay by making some changes, suggesting others, and questioning the writer about his meaning and intended effect. Most students will be surprised at the extensive editing Aaron suggests for an essay that looks so "finished." However, what is most instructive about this chapter is how much stronger the "finished" essay becomes. Aaron's editing of Thatcher's essay shows students how a revised sentence or a change in emphasis or tone makes the writer's intentions even clearer to his readers. It also shows students what happens when a piece of writing goes public. We have included a passage that Jane Aaron edited when she worked with the professional writer Gary Goshgarian to show how Aaron's editing helped simplify, clarify, and improve the emphasis of Goshgarian's essay.

After a brief introduction, the chapter begins with Aaron's description of an editor at work. Before students read this interesting account they should be asked what they know about the role of the editor in the writing/publishing process. There are many misconceptions about what editors do, and it is useful for students to sort out what they know from what they imagine to be the case. Aaron's overview of her work offers students a personal view of the editor's role as someone who sees the potential for better, clearer, and more convincing manuscripts. As Aaron writes: "An editor is a kind of messenger between writer and reader, representing each to the other. On the one hand, the editor helps the writer state his or her message as effectively as possible. On the other hand, the editor represents the typical reader for whom the piece of writing is intended, anticipating his or her needs for information, clarity, and readability."

John Clyde Thatcher's essay is complex and ambitious and required a complex editing job. Aaron deals with large problems, including organization and consistency of tone. It would be helpful for students to reread and discuss Thatcher's essay as it first appears in the book (pages 515–518). Aaron indicates that there are problems with Thatcher's sequencing of information and inconsistency in tone and purpose, necessitating substantial revisions.

Thatcher's commentary is particularly interesting, raising many issues to which students relate. For instance, Thatcher mentions his mild indignation at being edited. As he writes: "In the past I thought I personally was being edited, not the thing I'd written. After this experience I have learned that I am not being told I am inadequate but that my writing isn't as good as it might be." Thatcher comes to recognize that he needs to treat his writing as a craft: "My writing has always been an outlet for great emotion with little conscious thought toward form, balance, timing, and the things that make writing aesthetic. . . . I feel that too often I have been bowling my reader over with emotion and often have not been clear in an effort to be a better writer."

The questions on page 703 help students pull together the various pieces of material in this section. They allow students to understand Thatcher's purpose in his essay and the way in which he was able to strengthen that purpose through revision. The questions help students appreciate Aaron's comments on sequencing of information, inconsistency in tone, and changes for clarity and emphasis. Question 10, for instance, is a good exercise in close textual analysis: students are asked to study paragraph 2 of the original and revised essays and describe the differences between the two versions. Students might discover that Thatcher could have made further revisions in this paragraph and will probably enjoy playing the role of Thatcher's editor, suggesting to him that more changes are necessary. Students should be reminded, however, of what Aaron wrote in her description of her work: editing "requires an ability to work 'silently,' suspending one's own ideas instead of pushing them on the author. . . . Beyond grammar and spelling, few matters in writing are clear-cut: almost everything is a question of choice and of judgment, and judgment calls are endlessly debatable."

Throughout this chapter, and indeed through this part, we have tried to make the point to students that writing is a process of making choices and decisions. Our hope is that their choices are now more informed and that their confidence in themselves and in their decisions is more secure.

# A SUGGESTED SYLLABUS

*Student Writers at Work and in the company of other writers* is flexible enough to be taught in many ways. We present one possible sequence, encompassing an introduction and four large units that can be covered in fifteen weeks. Since each unit contains a variety of selections, instructors may choose and teach readings in different combinations. In each unit, student and professional essays are listed as they are paired in the book; although instructors may wish to teach either or both of the essays in a given pair, we have assumed for the purposes of this syllabus that the paired essays will be taught together.

## I. INTRODUCTION
### Course Time: One Week

"*Student Writers on Writing: An Overview*" (1–26) lets students "hear" the voices of prize-winning essayists as they discuss their writing processes; also have students fill out the questionnaire (25–26).

"*Revising Drafts*" (Chapter 1, 561-559) presents a detailed look at the composing processes of two prize-winning student writers. The class, guided by editorial comments, can examine Barbara Seidel's notes and rough draft along with her explanations of her intentions; then, guided by questions, they can analyze Brad Manning's drafts as he develops his essay from draft to final version.

## II. CREATING A VOICE
### Course Time: Four Weeks

We put this unit on voice first because students, as they talk about voice, begin to think about their writing — about the way they can use words to create emotions and personalities — and not merely about their ideas.

A voice can be created either by presenting a speaker or narrator who characterizes himself or by creating an implied perspective through tone, point of view, and vocabulary. Every essay has some sort of voice. The essays listed here are those in which voice is a distinctive feature: when we read each of these pieces, we inevitably summon up an image of the person speaking.

Students often think that the best way to write an essay is to try to efface their own personalities, to write in an impersonal, objective voice. Needless to say, this usually produces dull writing. We have found that an effective way to help students overcome dull writing is to begin the term by talking about how a writer creates the sense that a real person is speaking in an essay. Students can easily understand how to create a voice — simply ask the students to write a paragraph on a subject as if they were their fathers speaking and then to write one on the

112

same subject as if they were an eight-year-old girl speaking. Similarly, students can practice creating tones by writing, say, a sad and then an ecstatic description of high school graduation day.

Students sometimes feel that such exercises, however enjoyable, have little relevance to "real assignments." Yet as the Bedford Prize-winning essays in this section serve to show, excellent essays always use distinctive voices, tones, and point of view.

There are several ways to use the essays in this unit:

1. Students can study and then practice using one tone at a time, writing, say, an ironic, a bittersweet, and an impassioned essay, and then one point of view at a time. Students may surprise themselves by discovering that they write well in a tone and point of view they have never tried before — and even in a tone they thought they would never use. Some very hard-nosed people write quite sentimental essays, and bitter people write light and funny ones. After trying various tones and points of view, students can discuss which tones they feel most comfortable using and what other ones they might invent. Ultimately, the goal of imitating is for students to discover their own voices, their own tones, their own points of view.

2. Students can read several essays on the same subject written in different tones (Jennings and Hill write about "home," for example; you might also bring in James Baldwin, "Notes of a Native Son," for a very different view of "home"). Then each student can write an essay on that subject, developing his or her own tone.

3. Students can try writing a short essay using one point of view and then rewrite it using another. They can discuss how the essay changes.

4. Instead of starting with tone or point of view, you might start with a general discussion of how a writer creates a distinctive personality — a narrator — through words. To help students see what a narrator can contribute to an "objective," argumentative essay, begin the course with Ha Son Hi's and Mark Twain's essays. Once students have practiced creating strange narrators (animals, extraterrestrials, inanimate objects), they can begin to realize that even when they are trying to "be themselves," they still have to work hard to convey their own personality in words.

## A. Establishing a Distinctive Tone

1. Hard-edged, realistic tone
   Judy Jennings, "Second-Class Mom"
   Joan Didion, "On Going Home"
2. Impassioned tone
   Diane Kocour, "The Diet Industry Knows Best — Or Does It?"
   Thomas Jefferson, "The Declaration of Independence"
3. Ironic tone
   Allison Rolls, "Lady Diana: He Married the Wrong Woman"
   Alice Kahn, "Pianotherapy: Primal Pop"
4. Bittersweet tone
   William G. Hill, "Returning Home"
   Eudora Welty, "The Little Store"
5. Mixed tones
   Heather Ashley, "Leaving Vacita"
   E. B. White, "Once More to the Lake"

## B. Developing a Fresh Point of View

1. First person
   Beverly Dipo, "No Rainbows, No Roses"
   Oliver Sacks, "The Lost Mariner"

2. Second person (letter narration)
   Earnestine Johnson, "Thank You Miss Alice Walker: *The Color Purple*"
   Alice Walker, "A Letter of the Times, or Should This Sado-Masochism
   Be Saved?"
3. Third person
   Barbara Seidel, "A Tribute to My Father"
   Christopher Nolan, "Knife Used"

## C. Creating an Unusual Voice

Ha Song Hi, "From Xraxis to Dzreebo"
Mark Twain, "Letter to the Earth"


*"Peer Editing"* (Chapter 2, 600-641): Having encountered the variety of writers'
voices in the opening week(s) of the course as well as the fundamentals of the
composing and revising processes, students should be more than ready to learn
the principles and procedures of peer editing. (Note: Patrick Kinder Lewis's student
essay, peer edited in this chapter, also appears separately on this syllabus under
IV, "Building a Structure.")


### III. FOCUSING ON AN IDEA ABOUT A SUBJECT
### Course Time: Three Weeks

Often students will say that they have a general sense of the material they want
to include in an essay, but their ideas seem mushy and vague. The work of the
prize-winning writers in this section suggests several powerful methods for bringing ideas into focus. All of these methods transform ideas into new words and new
forms; they do not automatically produce a clear and precise focus. A writer who is
stuck, unable to express an idea, might have to explore several different contexts
or experiment with five or ten different metaphors or familiar images before finding
one that "works," that brings his or her ideas into focus.

The last method listed here — turning objects and events into symbols — is
most useful when a writer feels that he or she has gained insights from some
events (either personal experiences or public affairs) but cannot quite state those
insights. Such a writer might explore ways of describing those events as "symbolic"
— as meaningful and important — without worrying about stating the meaning
directly. To see that this is something students can do, look at Sisler's essay and
the explication that follows it. Patrick Kinder Lewis's essay "Five Minutes North of
Redding" provides another view of the use of symbols in essays.

## A. Drawing on Different Contexts or Frames of Reference

Bonnie Harris, "The Healing Power of Music"
Joyce Carol Oates, "On Boxing"

Thomas Leyba, "The Marfa Lights"
Tom Wolfe, "The Right Stuff"

## B. Using Metaphors to Define Ideas and Create Distinctions

Johnna Lynn Benson, "Rotten at the Core"
Lewis Thomas, "The World's Biggest Membrane"

Karen L. Kramer, "The Little Drummer Boys"
Richard Selzer, "Letter to a Young Surgeon

## C. Using Familiar Images to Clarify Complex Arguments

> Curtis Chang, "Streets of Gold: The Myth of the Model Minority"
> Aldous Huxley, "Words and Behavior"

## D. Assigning Symbolic Meaning to Objects and Events

> Paula Sisler, "The Water Lily"
> James Joyce, "Araby"

Since several of the student essays, notably Chang's, in this unit developed from intensely personal subject matter into expository argumentative essays, it is useful to teach Chapter 3 "Moving from Personal Experience to Exposition and Argument" (642–685) alongside these essays. If students have already studied Beverly Dipo's essay in unit II, they may find it instructive to trace her revision process in this chapter.

## IV. BUILDING A STRUCTURE
### Course Time: Five Weeks

Every writer has to decide how to arrange his or her material. Even if a writer is going to tell a story chronologically, he or she will have to decide how much space to devote to each event and how many clues to give readers about what is going to happen later in the story. Students sometimes think of structure as a form they are given, into which they must stuff their ideas. These prize-winning essays show how structures emerge from the topics and approaches of the writers and how structures can contribute to the power of essays. By their arrangement of their material, these writers tease us, leaving us in suspense; or surprise us, reversing direction suddenly; or create unusual connections between ideas and scenes; or produce musical effects, using repetitions to develop rhythms that subtly affect the way we read.

## A. Playing with the Audience's Expectations

1. Creating suspense
   Celeste Barrus, "Todd"
   William Carlos Williams, "The Use of Force"
2. Using a surprising opening
   James Seilsopour, "I Forgot the Words to the National Anthem"
   Richard Rodriguez, "Hunger of Memory"
3. Building to a surprising conclusion
   Todd Unruh, "No Respecter of Persons"
   Phyllis Rose, "Tools of Torture: An Essay on Beauty and Pain"
4. Surprising readers by revising in the middle of an essay
   Ann Louise Field, "The Sound of Angels"
   James Baldwin, "Notes of a Native Son"

   John Clyde Thatcher, "On Killing the Man"
   Doris Lessing, "The Old Chief Mshlanga"

## B. Creating Coherence (tying the parts of an essay together)

1. Using a generalization
   Terry L. Burns, "The Blanket Party"
   George Orwell, "Shooting an Elephant"
2. Using repeated elements
   Brad Manning, "Arm-Wrestling with My Father"
   Scott Russell Sanders, "The Inheritance of Tools"

Tor Valenza, "At Diane's"
Jo Goodwin Parker, "What Is Poverty?"
3. Using a narrative frame
John E. Mason, Jr., "Shared Birthdays"
Virginia Woolf, "The Death of the Moth"
4. Using the parts of another text
Margot Harrison, "Creative Transfiguration from the Death of a Moth"
Patricia Hampl, "Defying the Yapping Establishment: *Under the Eye of the Clock*"
5. Using a symbol
Patrick Kinder Lewis, "Five Minutes North of Redding"
Annie Dillard, "Death of a Moth"

## C. Taking Risks with Structure

An-Thu Quang Nguyen, "Tâi Con"
Maxine Hong Kingston, "The Woman Warrior"

*"Responding to Professional Editing"* (Chapter 4, 686–704): At this point in the course, the class may be ready to look closely at how a professional editor can help improve an essay. Students may appreciate how John Clyde Thatcher's prize-winning essay can be made even better through the assistance of a sensitive editor. The chapter may also help students understand the intentions of instructors, who offer useful advice as well as grades.

## V. DRAMATIZING AN ARGUMENT
### Course Time: Two Weeks

When students think of arguing, they focus largely on logic and ideas and tend to overlook the power of writing. The essays in this unit show that characters and scenes can be persuasive. If you wish to make argumentation a central part of your course, you can expand this unit considerably by adding to it other argumentative essays in this book. Techniques of argumentation are explored in all these student/professional pairings: Terry L. Burns/George Orwell; Curtis Chang/Aldous Huxley; Ha Song Hi/Mark Twain; Diane Kocour/Thomas Jefferson; and John Clyde Thatcher/Doris Lessing. Several other essays in the book that make strong arguments, though we have not focused our explications on their methods of argumentation, are those by James Baldwin, Maxine Hong Kingston, Phyllis Rose, and Jo Goodwin Parker.

## A. Creating a Character to Speak for the Author

David G. Landmann, "The House"
Francis Dana Barker Gage, "Sojourner Truth: And A'n't I a Woman?'

## B. Creating Opposing Characters to Portray the Sides of a Debate

Dianne Emminger, "The Exhibition"
Andrew Ward, "Yumbo"

## C. Dramatizing a Dilemma

Jill A. Savitt, "Decisions"
Nora Ephron, "The Boston Photographs"

# ELEMENTS OF COMPOSITION
## FOR THE STUDENT ESSAYS


## AUDIENCE

Celeste Barrus, "Todd"
Ann Louise Field, "The Sound of Angels"
Earnestine Johnson, "Thank You, Miss Alice Walker: *The Color Purple*"
James M. Seilsopour, "I Forgot the Words to the National Anthem"
John Clyde Thatcher, "On Killing the Man"
Todd Unruh, "No Respecter of Persons"


## PURPOSE

### To Explain

Bonnie Harris, "The Healing Power of Music"
Karen L. Kramer, "The Little Drummer Boys"
Thomas Leyba, "The Marfa Lights"

### To Inform

Celeste Barrus, "Todd"
Terry L. Burns, "The Blanket Party"
Judy Jennings, "Second-Class Mom"
David G. Landmann, "The House"
John Clyde Thatcher, "On Killing the Man"

### To Reflect

Heather Ashley, "Leaving Vacita"
Celeste Barrus, "Todd"
Johnna Lynn Benson, "Rotten at the Core"
Dianne Emminger, "The Exhibition"
Ann Louise Field, "The Sound of Angels"
William G. Hill, "Returning Home"
Earnestine Johnson, "Thank You, Miss Alice Walker: *The Color Purple*"
Patrick Kinder Lewis, "Five Minutes North of Redding"
Brad Manning, "Arm-Wrestling with My Father"
An-Thu Quang Nguyen, "Tâi Con"
Jill A. Savitt, "Decisions"
Barbara Seidel, "A Tribute to My Father"
Paula Sisler, "The Water Lily"
Tor Valenza, "At Diane's"

### To Entertain

Ha Song Hi, "From Xraxis to Dzreebo"
Karen L. Kramer, "The Little Drummer Boys"

Thomas Leyba, "The Marfa Lights"
Allison Rolls, "Lady Diana: He Married the Wrong Woman"
Tor Valenza, "At Diane's"

### To Analyze

Margot Harrison, "Creative Transfiguration from the Death of a Moth"
Thomas Leyba, "The Marfa Lights"

### To Criticize

Curtis Chang, "Streets of Gold: The Myth of the Model Minority"
Ha Song Hi, "From Xraxis to Dzreebo"
Diane Kocour, "The Diet Industry Knows Best — Or Does It?"
Todd Unruh, "No Respecter of Persons"

### To Satirize

Allison Rolls, "Lady Diana: He Married the Wrong Woman"

### To Convince or Persuade

Diane Kocour, "The Diet Industry Knows Best — Or Does It?"


## POINT OF VIEW

Terry L. Burns, "The Blanket Party"
Beverly Dipo, "No Rainbows, No Roses"
Ann Louise Field, "The Sound of Angels"
Ha Song Hi, "From Xraxis to Dzreebo"
Judy Jennings, "Second-Class Mom"
Earnestine Johnson, "Thank You, Miss Alice Walker: *The Color Purple*"
Karen L. Kramer, "The Little Drummer Boys"
John E. Mason, Jr., "Shared Birthdays"
An-Thu Quang Nguyen, "Tâi Con"
Jill A. Savitt, "Decisions"
Barbara Seidel, "A Tribute to My Father"


## TONE

### Personal

Heather Ashley, "Leaving Vacita"
Celeste Barrus, "Todd"
Dianne Emminger, "The Exhibition"
Ann Louise Field, "The Sound of Angels"
William G. Hill, "Returning Home"
Judy Jennings, "Second-Class Mom"
Earnestine Johnson, "Thank You, Miss Alice Walker: *The Color Purple*"
Karen L. Kramer, "The Little Drummer Boys"
Patrick Kinder Lewis, "Five Minutes North of Redding"
Brad Manning, "Arm-Wrestling with My Father"
An-Thu Quang Nguyen, "Tâi Con"
Barbara Seidel, "A Tribute to My Father"
James M. Seilsopour, "I Forgot the Words to the National Anthem"
Paula Sisler, "The Water Lily"
John Clyde Thatcher, "On Killing the Man"

**Impersonal**

Terry L. Burns, "The Blanket Party"
Margot Harrison, "Creative Transfiguration from the Death of a Moth"

**Humorous**

Ha Song Hi, "From Xraxis to Dzreebo"
Karen L. Kramer, "The Little Drummer Boys"
Allison Rolls, "Lady Diana: He Married the Wrong Woman"
Tor Valenza, "At Diane's"

**Ironical**

Ha Song Hi, "From Xraxis to Dzreebo"
Allison Rolls, "Lady Diana: He Married the Wrong Woman"
Todd Unruh, "No Respecter of Persons"

**Impassioned**

Diane Kocour, "The Diet Industry Knows Best — Or Does It?"

**Hard-edged (Realistic)**

Judy Jennings, "Second-Class Mom"

**Bittersweet**

Heather Ashley, "Leaving Vacita"
William G. Hill, "Returning Home"


## DICTION

**Formal**

Margot Harrison, "Creative Transfiguration from the Death of a Moth"
Diane Kocour, "The Diet Industry Knows Best — or Does It?"
Thomas Leyba, "The Marfa Lights"

**Informal**

Judy Jennings, "Second-Class Mom"
Brad Jennings, "Arm-Wrestling with My Father"
Allison Rolls, "Lady Diana: He Married the Wrong Woman"

**Dialect**

Ha Song Hi, "From Xraxis to Dzreebo"
An-Thu Quang Nguyen, "Tâi Con"

**Dialogue**

Heather Ashley, "Leaving Vacita"
Celeste Barrus, "Todd"
William G. Hill, "Returning Home"
David G. Landmann, "The House"
Patrick Kinder Lewis, "Five Minutes North of Redding"
An-Thu Quang Nguyen, "Tâi Con"
Jill A. Savitt, "Decisions"
James M. Seilsopour, "I Forgot the Words to the National Anthem"
Paula Sisler, "The Water Lily"
Todd Unruh, "No Respecter of Persons"

### Figurative Language

Johnna Lynn Benson, "Rotten at the Core"
Curtis Chang, "Streets of Gold: The Myth of the Model Minority"
Karen L. Kramer, "The Little Drummer Boys"
Patrick Kinder Lewis, "Five Minutes North of Redding"
Brad Manning, "Arm-Wrestling with My Father"
An-Thu Quang Nguyen, "Tâi Con"
Paula Sisler, "The Water Lily"

## EFFECTIVE BEGINNINGS

### Establishing the Importance of the Subject

Beverly Dipo, "No Rainbows, No Roses"
Curtis Chang, "Streets of Gold: The Myth of the Model Minority"
Thomas Leyba, "The Marfa Lights"

### Anecdote

Terry L. Burns, "The Blanket Party"
Ann Louise Field, "The Sound of Angels"
Diane Kocour, "The Diet Industry Knows Best — Or Does It?"
Brad Manning, "Arm-Wrestling with My Father"
Jill A. Savitt, "Decisions"
Barbara Seidel, "A Tribute to My Father"
Todd Unruh, "No Respecter of Persons"
Tor Valenza, "At Diane's"

### Quotation

Bonnie Harris, "The Healing Power of Music"
Thomas Leyba, "The Marfa Lights"

### Surprising Statement

Johnna Lynn Benson, "Rotten at the Core"
Beverly Dipo, "No Rainbows, No Roses"
Ha Song Hi, "From Xraxis to Dzreebo"
Judy Jennings, "Second-Class Mom"
Earnestine Johnson, "Thank You, Miss Alice Walker: *The Color Purple*"
James M. Seilsopour, "I Forgot the Words to the National Anthem"
Paula Sisler, "The Water Lily"

### Posing a Crucial Problem or Question

Margot Harrison, "Creative Transfiguration from the Death of a Moth"
Karen L. Kramer, "The Little Drummer Boys"
An-Thu Quang Nguyen, "Tâi Con"

## EFFECTIVE CONCLUSIONS

### Summarizing Essential Points

Ann Louise Field, "The Sound of Angels"
Patrick Kinder Lewis, "Five Minutes North of Redding"

### Framing (Returning to the Beginning)

Heather Ashley, "Leaving Vacita"
John E. Mason, Jr., "Shared Birthdays"

James M. Seilsopour, "I Forgot the Words to the National Anthem"
Tor Valenza, "At Diane's"

### Stimulating Further Discussion

Terry L. Burns, "The Blanket Party"
Curtis Chang, "Streets of Gold: The Myth of the Model Minority"
Ann Louise Field, "The Sound of Angels"

### Offering Recommendations, Solutions, or Answers

Bonnie Harris, "The Healing Power of Music"
Jill A. Savitt, "Decisions"

### Creating a Dramatic Example, Anecdote, or Phrase

Dianne Emminger, "The Exhibition"
Judy Jennings, "Second-Class Mom"
Diane Kocour, "The Diet Industry Knows Best — Or Does It?"
David G. Landmann, "The House"
Thomas Leyba, "The Marfa Lights"
An-Thu Quang Nguyen, "Tâi Con"
Allison Rolls, "Lady Diana: He Married the Wrong Woman"
Barbara Seidel, "A Tribute to My Father"
James M. Seilsopour, "I Forgot the Words to the National Anthem"
Paula Sisler, "The Water Lily"
John Clyde Thatcher, "On Killing the Man"

### Building to a Dramatic Conclusion

Celeste Barrus, "Todd"
Ha Song Hi, "From Xraxis to Dzreebo"
Todd Unruh, "No Respecter of Persons"


## EFFECTIVE PARAGRAPH

### Topic Sentence

Curtis Chang, "Streets of Gold: The Myth of the Model Minority"
Bonnie Harris, "The Healing Power of Music"
Margot Harrison, "Creative Transfiguration from the Death of a Moth"
Diane Kocour, "The Diet Industry Knows Best — Or Does It?"

### Coherence

Celeste Barrus, "Todd"
Terry L. Burns, "The Blanket Party"
Beverly Dipo, "No Rainbows, No Roses"
Margot Harrison, "Creative Transfiguration from the Death of a Moth"
Patrick Kinder Lewis, "Five Minutes North of Redding"
Thomas Leyba, "The Marfa Lights"
Brad Manning, "Arm-Wrestling with My Father"
John E. Mason, Jr., "Shared Birthdays"
Paula Sisler, "The Water Lily"
Tor Valenza, "At Diane's"

### Support

Curtis Chang, "Streets of Gold: The Myth of the Model Minority"
Ann Louise Field, "The Sound of Angels"
Bonnie Harris, "The Healing Power of Music"
Judy Jennings, "Second-Class Mom"

Diane Kocour, "The Diet Industry Knows Best — Or Does It?"
Thomas Leyba, "The Marfa Lights"

### Order (General to Specific)

Curtis Chang, "Streets of Gold: The Myth of the Model Minority"
Bonnie Harris, "The Healing Power of Music"
Diane Kocour, "The Diet Industry Knows Best — Or Does It?"
Thomas Leyba, "The Marfa Lights"

### Order (Specific to General)

Johnna Lynn Benson, "Rotten at the Core"
Terry L. Burns, "The Blanket Party"
Todd Unruh, "No Respecter of Persons"

### Order (Question and Answer)

Margot Harrison, "Creative Transfiguration from the Death of a Moth"
Karen L. Kramer, "The Little Drummer Boys"
An-Thu Quang Nguyen, "Tài Con"

### Order (Enumeration)

Curtis Chang, "Streets of Gold: The Myth of the Model Minority"
Bonnie Harris, "The Healing Power of Music"
An-Thu Quang Nguyen, "Tài Con"

### Transitions

Beverly Dipo, "No Rainbows, No Roses"
Bonnie Harris, "The Healing Power of Music"
Brad Manning, "Arm-Wrestling with My Father"
An-Thu Quang Nguyen, "Tài Con"


## INCORPORATING INFORMATION

### Quotation

Curtis Chang, "Streets of Gold: The Myth of the Model Minority"
Bonnie Harris, "The Healing Power of Music"
Margot Harrison, "Creative Transfiguration from the Death of a Moth"
Ha Song Hi, "From Xraxis to Dzreebo"
Thomas Leyba, "The Marfa Lights"
An-Thu Quang Nguyen, "Tài Con"
Jill A. Savitt, "Decisions"

### Paraphrase

Johnna Lynn Benson, "Rotten at the Core"
Curtis Chang, "Streets of Gold: The Myth of the Model Minority"
Bonnie Harris, "The Healing Power of Music"
Diane Kocour, "The Diet Industry Knows Best — Or Does It?"
Thomas Leyba, "The Marfa Lights"

### Data (Evidence)

Curtis Chang, "Streets of Gold: The Myth of the Model Minority"
Bonnie Harris, "The Healing Power of Music"
Margot Harrison, "Creative Transfiguration from the Death of a Moth"
Diane Kocour, "The Diet Industry Knows Best — Or Does It?"
Thomas Leyba, "The Marfa Lights"

## THEMATIC ARRANGEMENT
## FOR THE STUDENT AND PROFESSIONAL ESSAYS

### On Childhood

Heather Ashley, "Leaving Vacita"
Dianne Emminger, "The Exhibition"
Ann Louise Field, "The Sound of Angels"
William G. Hill, "Returning Home"
Brad Manning, Jr., "Arm-Wrestling with My Father"
John E. Mason, Jr., "Shared Birthdays"
John Clyde Thatcher, "On Killing the Man"

James Baldwin, "Notes of a Native Son"
Joan Didion, "On Going Home"
James Joyce, "Araby"
Maxine Hong Kingston, "The Woman Warrior"
Doris Lessing, "The Old Chief Mshlanga"
Christopher Nolan, "Knife Used"
Richard Rodriguez, "Hunger of Memory"
Scott Russell Sanders, "The Inheritance of Tools"
Eudora Welty, "The Little Store"
E. B. White, "Once More to the Lake"

### On Death

Celeste Barrus, "Todd"
Beverly Dipo, "No Rainbows, No Roses"
Margot Harrison, "Creative Transfiguration from the Death of a Moth"
Jill A. Savitt, "Decisions"
John Clyde Thatcher, "On Killing the Man"
Todd Unruh, "No Respecter of Persons"

James Baldwin, "Notes of a Native Son"
Annie Dillard, "Death of a Moth"
Nora Ephron, "The Boston Photographs"
George Orwell, "Shooting an Elephant"
Richard Selzer, "Letter to a Young Surgeon"
Tom Wolfe, "The Right Stuff"
Virginia Woolf, "The Death of the Moth"

### On the Family

Celeste Barrus, "Todd"
Ann Louise Field, "The Sound of Angels"
Judy Jennings, "Second-Class Mom"

David G. Landmann, "The House"
Brad Manning, "Arm-Wrestling with My Father"
Barbara Seidel, "A Tribute to My Father"
Paula Sisler, "The Water Lily"

James Baldwin, "Notes of a Native Son"
Joan Didion, "On Going Home"
James Joyce, "Araby"
Maxine Hong Kingston, "The Woman Warrior"
Christopher Nolan, "Knife Used"
Jo Goodwin Parker, "What Is Poverty?"
Richard Rodriguez, "Hunger of Memory"
Alice Walker, "A Letter of the Times, or Should This Sado-Masochism Be Saved?"
William Carlos Williams, "The Use of Force"

## On Fantasy

Heather Ashley, "Leaving Vacita"
Ha Song Hi, "From Xraxis to Dzreebo"
Thomas Leyba, "The Marfa Lights"

James Joyce, "Araby"
Mark Twain, "Letter to the Earth"
Alice Walker, "A Letter of the Times, or Should This Sado-Masochism Be Saved?"
E. B. White, "Once More to the Lake"

## On the Fine Arts

Dianne Emminger, "The Exhibition"
Bonnie Harris, "The Healing Power of Music"
Karen L. Kramer, "The Little Drummer Boys"

## On Food

Diane Kocour, "The Diet Industry Knows Best — Or Does It?"

Andrew Ward, "Yumbo"

## On Going Home

William G. Hill, "Returning Home"
John E. Mason, Jr., "Shared Birthdays"
An-Thu Quang Nguyen, "Tâi Con"
James M. Seilsopour, "I Forgot the Words to the National Anthem"

James Baldwin, "Notes of a Native Son"
Joan Didion, "On Going Home"
Richard Rodriguez, "Hunger of Memory"
Eudora Welty, "The Little Store"
E. B. White, "Once More to the Lake"

**On Health and Medicine**

Celeste Barrus, "Todd"
Beverly Dipo, "No Rainbows, No Roses"
Bonnie Harris, "The Healing Power of Music"
Diane Kocour, "The Diet Industry Knows Best — Or Does It?"

Oliver Sacks, "The Lost Mariner"
Richard Selzer, "Letter to a Young Surgeon"
William Carlos Williams, "The Use of Force"


**On Language**

Heather Ashley, "Leaving Vacita"
Curtis Chang, "Streets of Gold: The Myth of the Model Minority"
An-Thu Quang Nguyen, "Tâi Con"

Patricia Hampl, "Defying the Yapping Establishment: *Under the Eye of the Clock*"
Aldous Huxley, "Words and Behavior"
Maxine Hong Kingston, "The Woman Warrior"
Richard Rodriguez, "Hunger of Memory"
Andrew Ward, "Yumbo"


**On Literature**

Margot Harrison, "Creative Transfiguration from the Death of a Moth"
Earnestine Johnson, "Thank You, Miss Alice Walker: *The Color Purple*"

Patricia Hampl, "Defying the Yapping Establishment: *Under the Eye of the Clock*"
Richard Rodriguez, "Hunger of Memory"


**On Men**

Terry L. Burns, "The Blanket Party"
William G. Hill, "Returning Home"
Brad Manning, "Arm-Wrestling with My Father"
Barbara Seidel, "A Tribute to My Father"

Joyce Carol Oates, "On Boxing"
Scott Russell Sanders, "The Inheritance of Tools"
Tom Wolfe, "The Right Stuff"


**On Minorities**

Curtis Chang, "Streets of Gold: The Myth of the Model Minority"
Ha Song Hi, "From Xraxis to Dzreebo"
Earnestine Johnson, "Thank You, Miss Alice Walker: *The Color Purple*"
David G. Landmann, "The House"
An-Thu Quang Nguyen, "Tâi Con"
James M. Seilsopour, "I Forgot the Words to the National Anthem"

James Baldwin, "Notes of a Native Son"
Frances Dana Barker Gage, "Sojourner Truth: And A'n't I a Woman?"

Maxine Hong Kingston, "The Woman Warrior"
Doris Lessing, "The Old Chief Mshlanga"
Joyce Carol Oates, "On Boxing"
Richard Rodriguez, "Hunger of Memory"
Alice Walker, "A Letter of the Times, or Should This Sado-Masochism Be Saved?"

## On Music

Bonnie Harris, "The Healing Power of Music"
Karen L. Kramer, "The Little Drummer Boys"

## On Oppression

Terry L. Burns, "The Blanket Party"
Curtis Chang, "Streets of Gold: The Myth of the Model Minority"
Ha Song Hi, "From Xraxis to Dzreebo"
David G. Landmann, "The House"
An-Thu Quang Nguyen, "Tâi Con"
James M. Seilsopour, "I Forgot the Words to the National Anthem"

James Baldwin, "Notes of a Native Son"
Frances Dana Barker Gage, "Sojourner Truth: And A'n't I a Woman?"
Aldous Huxley, "Words and Behavior"
Thomas Jefferson, "The Declaration of Independence"
Maxine Hong Kingston, "The Woman Warrior"
Doris Lessing, "The Old Chief Mshlanga"
Christopher Nolan, "Knife Used"
George Orwell, "Shooting an Elephant"
Jo Goodwin Parker, "What Is Poverty?"
Richard Rodriguez, "Hunger of Memory"
Phyllis Rose, "Tools of Torture: An Essay on Beauty and Pain"
Alice Walker, "A Letter of the Times, or Should This Sado-Masochism Be Saved?"

## On Parents

Celeste Barrus, "Todd"
Judy Jennings, "Second-Class Mom"
Brad Manning, "Arm-Wrestling with My Father"
Barbara Seidel, "A Tribute to My Father"
Paula Sisler, "The Water Lily"

James Baldwin, "Notes of a Native Son"
Joan Didion, "On Going Home"
Maxine Hong Kingston, "The Woman Warrior"
Christopher Nolan, "Knife Used"
Scott Russell Sanders, "The Inheritance of Tools"
E. B. White, "Once More to the Lake"
William Carlos Williams, "The Use of Force"

## On People

Celeste Barrus, "Todd"
Terry L. Burns, "The Blanket Party"
Curtis Chang, "Streets of Gold: The Myth of the Model Minority"

Dianne Emminger, "The Exhibition"
William G. Hill, "Returning Home"
Judy Jennings, "Second-Class Mom"
Diane Kocour, "The Diet Industry Knows Best — Or Does It?"
Karen L. Kramer, "The Little Drummer Boys"
An-Thu Quang Nguyen, "Tâi Con"
Jill A. Savitt, "Decisions"
James M. Seilsopour, "I Forgot the Words to the National Anthem"
Todd Unruh, "No Respecter of Persons"
Barbara Seidel, "A Tribute to My Father"

James Baldwin, "Notes of a Native Son"
Joan Didion, "On Going Home"
Nora Ephron, "The Boston Photographs"
Maxine Hong Kingston, "The Woman Warrior"
Doris Lessing, "The Old Chief Mshlanga"
Phyllis Rose, "Tools of Torture: An Essay on Beauty and Pain"
E. B. White, "Once More to the Lake"
William Carlos Williams, "The Use of Force"


## On Places

Heather Ashley, "Leaving Vacita"
Dianne Emminger, "The Exhibition"
William G. Hill, "Returning Home"
David G. Landmann, "The House"
Doris Lessing, "The Old Chief Mshlanga"
Thomas Leyba, "The Marfa Lights"
John E. Mason, Jr., "Shared Birthdays"
An-Thu Quang Nguyen, "Tâi Con"
Todd Unruh, "No Respecter of Persons"
Tor Valenza, "At Diane's"

James Joyce, "Araby"
Christopher Nolan, "Knife Used"
George Orwell, "Shooting an Elephant"
Lewis Thomas, "The World's Biggest Membrane"
Andrew Ward, "Yumbo"
Eudora Welty, "The Little Store"
E. B. White, "Once More to the Lake"


## On Poverty

Ann Louise Field, "The Sound of Angels"
Ha Song Hi, "From Xraxis to Dzreebo"
David G. Landmann, "The House"

Jo Goodwin Parker, "What Is Poverty?"
Richard Rodriguez, "Hunger of Memory"


## On Regional Identity

Ann Louise Field, "The Sound of Angels"
William G. Hill, "Returning Home"
David G. Landmann, "The House"

Thomas Leyba, "The Marfa Lights"
An-Thu Quang Nguyen, "Tâi Con"
James M. Seilsopour, "I Forgot the Words to the National Anthem"
John Clyde Thatcher, "On Killing the Man"
Tor Valenza, "At Diane's"

Maxine Hong Kingston, "The Woman Warrior"
Doris Lessing, "The Old Chief Mshlanga"
Christopher Nolan, "Knife Used"
George Orwell, "Shooting an Elephant"
Eudora Welty, "The Little Store"
E. B. White, "Once More to the Lake"

## On Rituals

Heather Ashley, "Leaving Vacita"
Terry L. Burns, "The Blanket Party"
Brad Manning, "Arm-Wrestling with My Father"
John E. Mason, Jr., "Shared Birthdays"
Allison Rolls, "Lady Diana: He Married the Wrong Woman"
John Clyde Thatcher, "On Killing the Man"
Todd Unruh, "No Respecter of Persons"

James Baldwin, "Notes of a Native Son"
Annie Dillard, "Death of a Moth"
Joyce Carol Oates, "On Boxing"
Phyllis Rose, "Tools of Torture: An Essay on Beauty and Pain"
Scott Russell Sanders, "The Inheritance of Tools"
E. B. White, "Once More to the Lake"
Tom Wolfe, "The Right Stuff"

## On Rural America

Ann Louise Field, "The Sound of Angels"
William G. Hill, "Returning Home"
Patrick Kinder Lewis, "Five Minutes North of Redding"
Thomas Leyba, "The Marfa Lights"
John Clyde Thatcher, "On Killing the Man"

Jo Goodwin Parker, "What Is Poverty?"
Eudora Welty, "The Little Store"
E. B. White, "Once More to the Lake"

## On Self-Identity

Johnna Lynn Benson, "Rotten at the Core"
Curtis Chang, "Streets of Gold: The Myth of the Model Minority"
William G. Hill, "Returning Home"
Earnestine Johnson, "Thank You, Miss Alice Walker: *The Color Purple*"
Diane Kocour, "The Diet Industry Knows Best — Or Does It?"
Patrick Kinder Lewis, "Five Minutes North of Redding"
Brad Manning, "Arm-Wrestling with My Father"
An-Thu Quang Nguyen, "Tâi Con"
Jill A. Savitt, "Decisions"
James M. Seilsopour, "I Forgot the Words to the National Anthem"
Paula Sisler, "The Water Lily"

John Clyde Thatcher, "On Killing the Man"
Todd Unruh, "No Respecter of Persons"
Tor Valenza, "At Diane's"

Joan Didion, "On Going Home"
Frances Dana Barker Gage, "Sojourner Truth: And A'n't I a Woman?"
Aldous Huxley, "Words and Behavior"
Alice Kahn, "Pianotherapy: Primal Pop"
Doris Lessing, "The Old Chief Mshlanga"
Christopher Nolan, "Knife Used"
George Orwell, "Shooting an Elephant"
Richard Rodriguez, "Hunger of Memory"
Oliver Sacks, "The Lost Mariner"
Richard Selzer, "Letter to a Young Surgeon"
Alice Walker, "A Letter of the Times, or Should This Sado-Masochism Be Saved?"
William Carlos Williams, "The Use of Force"


## On Violence

Terry L. Burns, "The Blanket Party"
Brad Manning, "Arm-Wrestling with My Father"
An-Thu Quang Nguyen, "Tâi Con"
Jill A. Savitt, "Decisions"
James M. Seilsopour, "I Forgot the Words to the National Anthem"
John Clyde Thatcher, "On Killing the Man"

James Baldwin, "Notes of a Native Son"
Annie Dillard, "Death of a Moth"
Nora Ephron, "The Boston Photographs"
Aldous Huxley, "Words and Behavior"
Maxine Hong Kingston, "The Woman Warrior"
Doris Lessing, "The Old Chief Mshlanga"
Joyce Carol Oates, "On Boxing"
George Orwell, "Shooting an Elephant!"
Phyllis Rose, "Tools of Torture: An Essay on Beauty and Pain"
Alice Walker, "A Letter of the Times, or Should This Sado-Masochism Be Saved?"
William Carlos Williams, "The Use of Force"
Virginia Woolf, "The Death of the Moth"


## On War

Terry L. Burns, "The Blanket Party"
An-Thu Quang Nguyen, "Tâi Con"

Aldous Huxley, "Words and Behavior"


## On Women

Judy Jennings, "Second-Class Mom"
Earnestine Johnson, "Thank You Miss Alice Walker: *The Color Purple*"
Diane Kocour, "The Diet Industry Knows Best — Or Does It?"
Allison Rolls, "Lady Diana: He Married the Wrong Woman"

Frances Dana Barker Gage, "Sojourner Truth: And A'n't I a Woman?"
Maxine Hong Kingston, "The Woman Warrior"

Phyllis Rose, "Tools of Torture: An Essay on Beauty and Pain"
Alice Walker, "A Letter of the Times, or Should This Sado-Masochism Be Saved?"

## On Working

Beverly Dipo, "No Rainbows, No Roses"
Bonnie Harris, "The Healing Power of Music"
Karen L. Kramer, "The Little Drummer Boys"
Jill A. Savitt, "Decisions"

Nora Ephron, "The Boston Photographs"
Joyce Carol Oates, "On Boxing"
George Orwell, "Shooting an Elephant"
Scott Russell Sanders, "The Inheritance of Tools"
Richard Selzer, "Letter to a Young Surgeon"
Andrew Ward, "Yumbo"
Tom Wolfe, "The Right Stuff"

## Just Published!

# A WRITER'S REFERENCE

**Diana Hacker,** *Prince Georges Community College*

**1989/paper/224 pages/*Exercises to Accompany A Writer's Reference***

Designed to be a brief, convenient reference, this handbook's unique physical format makes it remarkably easy to consult. The combed plastic binding allows the book to lie flat, while tabbed section dividers let students quickly flip to the section they want. Based on the bestselling second edition of *Rules for Writers, A Writer's Reference* covers all the topics for which students consult a handbook—the conventions of grammar and usage, documentation, as well as the writing process.

## *Just Published!*

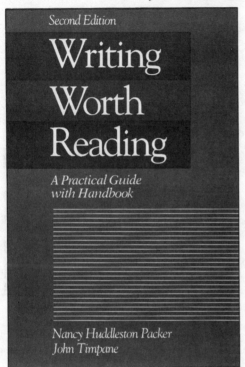

Second Edition

# Writing Worth Reading

*A Practical Guide with Handbook*

*Nancy Huddleston Packer*
*John Timpane*

## WRITING WORTH READING: A Practical Guide with Handbook, Second Edition

**Nancy Huddleston Packer**, *Stanford University*
**John Timpane**, *Lafayette College*

**1989/paper/624 pages/Instructor's Manual**

This second edition of a highly regarded rhetoric and handbook features increased emphasis on critical thinking and reading skills necessary for serious work at the college level. Includes an expanded handbook and strengthened chapters on research and report writing, while it retains the authors' engaging and witty writing style.

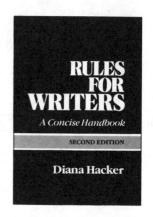